offering ... *to enrich everyday living*

"Your word is a lamp to my feet
and a light to my path."
Psalm 119:105

The fruit of the Spirit is
love, joy, peace, patience, kindness, generosity,
faithfulness, gentleness, and self-control.

— Galatians 5:22–23a

Spirit Life

Living the Fruit of God's Spirit

Christopher Page

Path Books
A LIGHT TO MY PATH

ABC Publishing, Anglican Book Centre
General Synod of the Anglican Church of Canada
80 Hayden Street, Toronto, Ontario, Canada M4Y 3G2
abcpublishing@national.anglican.ca
www.abcpublishing.com www.pathbooks.com

Text set in ITC Legacy Serif and Dickens Script
Cover and text design by Jane Thornton
Cover photo: Wayne & Linda Bonnett/ Photodisc/Getty Images

Library and Archives Canada Cataloguing in Publication
Page, Christopher, 1954-

Spirit life : living the fruit of God's spirit / Christopher Page.
ISBN 978-1-55126-496-7
ISBN 1-55126-496-X

1. Fruit of the Spirit. 2. Christian life—Anglican authors.
3. Spirituality. I. Title.

BV4501.3.P332 2007   234'.13   C2007-904058-6

Printed in Canada

Contents

For Rachel and Naomi,
in whom I find so many of the
fruit of God's Spirit

Introduction

Working in the church often includes participating in the inevitable transition that occurs as physical life comes to an end. Recently, I had a week that included three memorial services. Each of these services celebrated the life of a person who had died after living a long, faith-filled life. They were not famous or powerful people. None of them had made a tremendous public impact upon the world. But each of these lives was characterized by many of those qualities we would think are among the best characteristics to be found in any human being.

As I went through this week of celebrating the lives of those who had died, I became aware that an era was coming to an end. These people were all my parents' peers. They represent the generation that has gone ahead of my generation. As I reflected upon the fact that my generation will be the next to pass, I began to wonder where my children and their peers will look to find examples of the best qualities of human nature. Who in my generation has picked up the torch of the previous generation to bear testimony to life lived according to the highest and most true values of which humans are capable? Where will those who are moving into adulthood look for a vision of what it means to be truly human?

The book you are holding in your hands is a book about vision. The pages that follow attempt to present a Christian vision of what it might mean to be human. What will a truly and deeply human life look like? What are those qualities that characterize the best we can hope for in a human being?

Occasionally we hear particular types of behaviour excused with the question, "Well, what do you expect, he's only human?"

This seems to suggest that being human means behaving in a way that falls below a quality of character and conduct for which we might hope. There are many places we might look to find visions of what it means to live in a way that is less than human. The world provides no shortage of examples of lives lived according to a sub-human standard. But where might we find a vision of a richly authentic human way of being?

In the scriptures of the Christian tradition we are presented with an extraordinarily exalted vision of human conduct. We are challenged to explore and live up to the highest standard of human living. In the chapters that follow this introduction we will explore the high calling of the Christian vision for human life. We will attempt to find ways in which God makes it possible for us to live more closely in tune with that reality for which we were created.

The most fundamental reality the Bible tells us about the human creation is that we humans were created "in the image of God." This is the first thing we need to know about our human condition. Everything flows from the reality of our created identity. We are those beings who are created "in the image of God." To be created "in the image of God" means there is something within us that bears the imprint of the Eternal. There is that within us which carries some resemblance to God. The more we can live truly human lives, the more deeply we will come to reflect that One in whose image we were originally created. The closer we come to that One by whom we were created, the more we will come to reflect the One whose image we bear.

The purpose of human existence is to come back into tune with the "image of God" that is our birthright as God's children. We fulfill our destiny as beings created by God, to the degree that we are able to align ourselves with our nature as it truly is. This is not the same as simply conforming to a long list of rules and regulations. It is more a matter of finding the true flow of the stream and allowing the little boat of our lives to conform to the contours of reality as it has been created.

We seek in this exploration of the human condition to uncover a true picture of that which is steady, permanent, and most real in human nature. We are looking for a vision of what a human being might truly look like when that being is living in tune with his or her true nature. We are trying to discover how the human part of creation is actually designed to operate.

It is imperative that we discover deeper, more authentic ways of being human. We are all tragically familiar with the devastation that is caused by human beings when we choose to live out of tune with our truest and deepest nature. Our planet suffers the grievous effects of the human determination to live by something less than that which is most truly human. The human community is torn apart by our unwillingness to allow our spirits to flow with the true nature of our created identity. Our own personal lives are impoverished and tortured by our failure to see and to follow the way creation is designed to unfold.

The world cries out for a vision of what it means for human beings to live together in ways that are truly life-giving. Our planet aches for humans to live more authentically and genuinely in relationship to the non-human community with which we share our home. Every generation needs to revision for itself what it means to be human. This does not mean that we will discover new ways of being human. The ways of being truly human have existed from that moment when the first human received from God the breath of life. To revision what it means to be human means identifying those ancient truths about the human condition and translating them with freshness and vigor into contemporary terms.

The goal of this book is to reach back into the ancient wisdom of Christian tradition and find a renewed vision of the human enterprise. In these pages we will attempt to renew our vision of what it means to be human. We will raise up a light that can shine with renewed brightness guiding us toward a more authentic way of being human. We will discover deep truths of our human nature and the ways God has given us to live more fully in tune with the gift of life that has been entrusted to us.

Beyond Nice

Galatians 5:16

It is a dangerous question, but one worth asking: what does a Christian life look like?

The danger lies in the risk that, having described how a Christian life might look, we turn the description into a set of rules by which we attempt to govern human behaviour. Humans seem to have a deep need to create rules. We find security in the illusion that we understand how the game is to be played. We want to know how to win, who measures up and who falls short. We believe that life will work well if we obey the rules and things will go badly for those who disobey. We want life to be tidy.

Life, however, seldom cooperates with our desire for neatness. The complexities of human existence cannot easily be reduced to do's and don'ts. Most parents have heard their children say, "It's not fair." True — life is not fair. In the Hebrew psalms the writer complains constantly that the wicked prosper and the righteous appear to be punished by life. The entire book of Job makes the single point that God does not operate according to the prescriptions of human standards and judgements.

It often appears that there are no hard and fast rules that govern anything in life. There is an enormous amount of chance in the human condition. In hurricane season, the news reports that horrific storm winds and high seas are devastating the Caribbean and heading for Cuba. Then we hear that the hurricane has "wobbled," and suddenly Cuba is spared and the residents of Alabama are lashed by a ferocious storm. No one can predict. Certainly, no one can control the mighty forces of nature.

In the Christian understanding, when God desired to be most fully revealed in human history, God did not write down a list of prescriptions. Words fixed on paper cannot adapt to the changeable nature of human reality. God's self-revelation came instead in the form of a living Word incarnate in the existence of one person. Jesus interacted with the uncertain circumstances of human existence and responded to the situations of human beings as he encountered them. Jesus showed the life of God involved in the messy, complicated circumstances of the human condition.

Jesus did not attempt to govern the lives of his followers using a tidy list of rules. He did not go up a mountain and return with Ten Commandments carved in stone to pass on from generation to generation. Jesus did not leave a single written document. As far as we can discern from the gospel accounts, he never even instructed anyone to write down any of his words or to record in any way the things he said or did. How could Jesus have been so careless? Surely, he wanted to preserve his teaching for posterity and to keep his followers on the right path.

Jesus knew something we tend to forget. He knew that faith cannot be based on adherence to an external code of conduct. Jesus knew that, just as his first followers needed to walk and live in his presence, so those who would come after his first disciples would need that same experience. So we are given the opportunity not to follow a set of rules, but to live in relationship with the living presence of God known to us through Christ. Christian life is based on presence rather than precept. At the end of Matthew's gospel, Jesus' last words to his followers, before his physical departure, were, "Remember, I am with you always." We need to experience the reality of Jesus' presence if we hope to live the fullness of life for which we were created.

Following closely the Spirit of Jesus, Paul the first great teacher of Christian faith, recognized that the law cannot bring life. Paul says, "the law brings wrath" (Romans 4:15). The law brings separation, darkness, anger, despair, a sense of loss. Rules do not deepen authentic human living. The law cannot open us to our true nature. Law creates boundaries, draws lines in the sand, and establishes unhealthy comparisons between people. Law cannot bring the spontaneity and freedom for which we long, and for which we were originally created.

Jesus is portrayed in the gospels as being constantly assaulted by the problem of the law. The religious officials of his day wanted Jesus to tune his song of love to the instrument of their legalism. They demanded that Jesus follow the strict code of their religious and moral observance. When Jesus failed to fulfill the demands of religion, the establishment of his day determined that he was a dangerous influence and must be destroyed.

Despite his problems with the law, Jesus himself said that he had come not to "abolish" the law. The law can give "helpful information"[1] about how to live life. But the law cannot give us life. So although he did not intend to do away with the law, Jesus did desire to "fulfill" the law (Matthew 5:17). He came to demonstrate the true meaning of the law, to uncover the essence of the law. The religious officials of his day focused on the letter of the law. Jesus paid attention to the purpose of the law.

When we focus on the letter of the law, we focus our attention on human behaviour and conduct. We emphasize the things people do. We place ourselves in judgement upon the behaviour of others. The letter of the law gives us the illusion that we can judge people's behaviour on the clear basis of right and wrong, according to how their behaviour corresponds, or fails to correspond, to our list of approved and disapproved actions. But such a view does not take into consideration the deep complexities of the human condition. In fact, the law exists to provoke a crisis that compels us to look beyond the law. Rowan Williams

---

1   Richard Rohr, *Everything Belongs: The Gift of Contemplative Prayer* (New York: Crossroad, 1999), p. 99.

says that through the law, "God provokes crisis to destroy our self-deceiving trust in Law."[2] We need something more alive and vital than law.

We need to focus our attention beyond the law to its source. Looking beyond the law, we pay less attention to human conduct and more attention to the living presence of God known to us in the person of Jesus Christ. Jesus was primarily concerned with the condition of the human heart and only secondarily with human conduct. Jesus said, "For out of the heart come evil intentions, murder, adultery, fornication, theft, false witness, slander" (Matthew 15:19). So our focus needs to be on the heart first. We only focus on behaviour because behaviour reveals the condition of the heart. If behaviour is going to be changed, it will be because the human heart has changed.

In place of rules and regulations the New Testament gives us a number of lists of qualities the authors believe will come to characterize the lives of those who walk in the Spirit of Christ. The point of these lists is never to focus on the qualities themselves. We will always misunderstand Christian faith and life if we aspire to emulate only the Christian qualities we find described in the New Testament.

One of the places Paul most clearly spells out the characteristics that he anticipates he might find in the life of a follower of Jesus Christ is in Galatians 5:22–23, a passage commonly known as "The Fruit of the Spirit." It is essential to read these two verses in the context in which they appear. Paul states clearly in 5:16, leading up to his description of "the fruit of the Spirit," that in verses 22 and 23 he is describing what life looks like when it is

---

2 Rowan Williams, *The Wound of Knowledge: A Theological History from the New Testament to Luther and St. John of the Cross* (Eugene, Oregon: Wipf and Stock, 2000), p.6.

lived "by the Spirit." This is not life lived by human effort. Paul is not challenging us to exert our will-power to make ourselves more like the people he describes. Paul is giving us a vision of how a life lived by the Spirit will come to resemble God's life.

There is an important translation challenge in Galatians 5:16. In most translations this verse says something like, "Live by the Spirit, I say, and do not gratify the desires of the flesh." This sounds like two commands: one, "live by the Spirit," and two, "do not gratify the desires of the flesh." But in fact, this picture does not accurately reflect the intention of the Greek. The verb translated "do not gratify the desires" is an emphatic future negative conditional tense. Paul is making an emphatic statement that is conditional upon the fulfillment of the previous statement. Paul is saying, "Live by the Spirit, I say, and **then** you will not gratify the desires of the flesh."

J. B. Phillips captures the sense of the Greek beautifully in his translation when he has Paul say, "Here is my advice. Live your whole life in the Spirit and you will not satisfy the desires of your lower nature." Paul does not challenge us to become better people. He does not instruct us to discipline ourselves to live more morally upright lives. He simply tells us that, if we stay connected to God, this is what our lives will look like. Then he paints the extraordinary picture of Christian life we call "the fruit of the Spirit."

If we stay connected to God's Spirit, our lives will be characterized by "love, joy, peace, patience, kindness, generosity, faithfulness, gentleness, and self-control." If we stay connected to God, we will become more like the God to whom we are connected. Our lives tend to take the shape of whatever we place at the centre of our lives.

In Matthew's gospel, Jesus expresses the challenge of the Christian life in the most stark terms possible. He says, simply, "Be perfect, therefore, as your heavenly Father is perfect" (Matthew 5:48). If you think that self-effort and hard work will enable you to fulfill this vision, you have greater optimism about your abilities than I have about mine.

The problem for law-keepers is that their vision is too small. They think that being Christian means simply being a nice person. They think that being Christian means that you don't swear and don't get drunk all the time and that you try to stay with a single partner. Those are not bad things, but they are a far cry from the extraordinarily exalted vision God has for our lives. As followers of Christ, we will never be content to settle for the life of a conventionally good person.

As we explore the fruit of the Spirit that God desires to grow in our lives, we will discover that we are called to something much greater than niceness. We are called to something much deeper and more challenging than conventional morality. It is relatively easy to be a decent person. You do not need to bother with Christianity or religion or any kind of faith in order to be a nice person. The world is full of nice people. There may well be many more much nicer people outside of church than there are inside. But we are called to something much greater than niceness.

As we examine the fruit of the Spirit Paul describes, we will discover something about what it means to live beyond niceness. We will explore what it means to allow God's life to be born in us. We will uncover the extraordinary challenge of being the true manifestation of God.

God's Vision For Our Lives

Galatians 5:16

Before we examine the "the fruit of the Spirit" in detail, we need to understand how Christian faith views the human condition. In Galatians 5:16–17 Paul summarizes the essential nature of the human situation. Human beings are caught in a dilemma. We live in the midst of an irreconcilable tension; a profound conflict characterizes our very nature. Paul says,

> Live by the Spirit, I say, and do not gratify the desires of the flesh. For what the flesh desires is opposed to the Spirit, and what the Spirit desires is opposed to the flesh; for these are opposed to each other, to prevent you from doing what you want (Galatians 5:16–17).

It is important in reading these verses to understand Paul's terminology. He speaks of "Spirit" on the one hand and "flesh" on the other hand. The Greek word translated "flesh" is *sarx*. In this context it does not mean body. J. B. Phillips captures the sense in which Paul is using this term in his translation when he says,

> Live your whole life in the Spirit and you will not satisfy the desires of your **lower nature**. For the whole energy of the **lower nature** is set against the Spirit, while the whole power of the Spirit is contrary to the **lower nature**.

We are divided people. We have a "lower nature" and we have a "Spirit nature." As long as we live in this world, these two natures will remain at war with one another. In Romans, Paul describes this battle, saying in Phillip's translation,

> My own behaviour baffles me. For I find myself doing what I really loathe but not doing what I really want to do. Yet surely if I do things that I really don't want to do, I am admitting that I really agree that the Law is good. But it cannot be said that 'I' am doing them at all—it must be sin that has made its home in my nature. And, indeed, I know from experience that the carnal side of my being can scarcely be called the home of God.

So there is a self within us that is "the home of God." And there is a self within us that is constantly opposed to God. We are flesh, and we are Spirit. The question of the Christian life is, With which of these two natures am I going to align myself? Will I live by the flesh, following the dictates of my lower nature? Or will I "live by the Spirit," following the gravitation from above? If I choose to live by my lower nature, I choose to live by something less than I am created to be.

Bede Griffiths describes the tension between flesh and Spirit, saying, "If the soul identifies itself with the body, it becomes enclosed in its separate existence, but if it opens itself to the Spirit, it can transcend its separate individuality and realize its identity with the Spirit."[3] The soul is the human power that has the capacity to move toward the physical or the spiritual. When the soul "identifies itself with the body," it becomes "enclosed" in an illusory state that Paul calls "flesh."

The flesh is not my true self. Flesh is a small self within my being, and when I follow this small self, I live contrary to my true and deep nature. This is when I, and all people, run into problems.

---

3   Bede Griffiths, *Return to the Center* (Springfield, Illinois: Templegate, 1976), p. 131.

It is important to see the true nature of this self that is less than I was created to be. Paul describes this aspect of my personality by giving a list of its characteristic behaviours. Paul says, "Now the works of the flesh are obvious: fornication, impurity, licentiousness, idolatry, sorcery, enmities, strife, jealousy, anger, quarrels, dissensions, factions, envy, drunkenness, carousing" (Galatians 5:18–21).

At the end of this list Paul adds the words, "and things like these." Paul does not want us to get hung up on the list. The list is simply representative. The important thing to see is what human quality these behaviours of our small self have in common.

These behaviours all share the fundamental characteristic that the small self always puts itself first without any consideration for the consequences in the lives of others. For the small self I am always the centre of my own little universe. And it is a very small universe, without any room for anyone but myself and perhaps those few people who meet my needs and fulfill my wishes. The small self defines the world in terms of my needs, my desires, my wants, my likes and dislikes.

And, because the small self always views life in terms of my needs, he always feels threatened and insecure. He lives with his defences up. He is always on his guard. He sees the world in terms of those who are for him and those who are against him. He is insecure, threatened, anxious, and always fearful. He spends his entire life trying to convince himself that he is significant and strong, because he never succeeds. He creates drama wherever he goes, in an attempt to convince himself that his life is really important and meaningful.

This small self is sometimes called the "ego" or the "false self." It is not "false" in the sense that it is bad. It is "false" in the sense that it is something much less than my true self. When we see in our lives the kinds of behaviours that Paul talks about in Galatians 5:18–21, we need to recognize that we are living a lie. We are living according to something less than our true nature.

We were not created for "fornication, impurity, licentiousness, idolatry, sorcery, enmities, strife, jealousy, anger, quarrels, dissensions, factions, envy, drunkenness, carousing." These behaviours indicate that we have descended from the exalted heights of our true created nature and are not fulfilling our true destiny.

William Shannon, describing Thomas Merton's understanding of "the false self," says, "Our false selves exist, but at the level of illusion; they have no ultimate reality. They are the selves we imagine we are, not the selves that we are at our center."[4] It is a tragedy when human beings live as something less than they were created to be. But it is important not to beat ourselves up about this tragedy. The behaviours of the small self are not an indication that we are evil. They merely indicate that we are living out of tune with what is most true about ourselves. My small self developed his behaviours for good reasons. He developed his self-serving behaviours because he was scared.

We were not created with a small self. It came into existence when we began to feel vulnerable. In developing a small self we were attempting to deal with the world, to help ourselves cope with the sense of danger and separation that the world seemed to present.

I remember as a small boy, probably not yet six, sitting precariously balanced on a neighbour's narrow little black iron fence. There were four other children with me. I do not remember what we were talking about at the time, but I remember a sudden feeling of separation that came over me. Suddenly, I knew that we were all different people. We did not seem to belong to one another. I began to feel small, uncertain, and vulnerable. I knew in that instant that I needed to do something to make myself

---

4   William Shannon, *Thomas Merton's Paradise Journey: Writings on Contemplation* (Cincinnati, Ohio: St. Anthony Messenger, 2000), p. 54.

bigger. I needed to say something that would make an impression on my peers. I needed to establish my territory and fight for my place in the world.

When we feel insecure, the small self has been taught to fight back, to stick up for itself. When the small self feels threatened, it knows that it needs to get angry. So the world of the small self is filled with "enmities, strife, jealousy, anger, quarrels, dissensions, factions."

The small self lives by comparisons. The small self knows who is the biggest, who is the smartest, richest, best looking, and most popular. The small self is frequently consumed with envy because the small self knows that in any comparison he will always come up short, be found wanting, be inadequate. The world can never give the small self enough to feel secure. So the small self moves from the poison of envy to sadness, discontent, and often to depression.

When we feel depressed or depleted, the small self has been taught to go and seek some kind of thrill as a reward for the awful drudgery of life. So we try "fornication, impurity, licentiousness ... drunkenness, carousing." When God does not seem to be making life run as smoothly as we would like, the small self goes out and finds some other reward, some other object of worship. So the small self falls prey to a great variety of the world's "idolatry."

The problem with allowing this small self to direct our lives is that, when the small self is in charge, we will never fulfill the ultimate goal of our human destiny. Paul says, "those who do such things will not inherit the kingdom of God." He is not saying here that those who do these things will never go to heaven. Heaven is not the issue here. Paul is concerned in this passage with how we live full, healthy human lives in the present, not with gaining some eternal reward in the great hereafter.

Paul is saying that those who live according to the small self will never live in tune with their true nature. We were created to live in alignment with the God who created us. We were created to live by the light, truth, love, and compassion of God. That is who we are. When we live according to the small self, we are aligning ourselves with an energy force that is, in fact, working against the fulfillment of our true being.

It is a crucial first step in the spiritual life to recognize that this small self is not who we are. It is not our created identity. This is not the being God gave us at the beginning. Paul says, "if I do things that I really don't want to do ... it cannot be said that 'I' am doing them at all." So this small-self "I" is not the "I" that I truly am. This vulnerable little person inside of me is a pretender, a coping mechanism, that I put in place to deal with life before I was able to develop better coping mechanisms. We need to see this small "I" for what it is and not allow ourselves to think that this is who we really are. We must avoid at all costs making an identity out of this small "I."

Alcoholics Anonymous has done an enormous amount of good in our society. There is probably not another social movement in modern times that has done more to bring sanity and health into people's lives. I have never been to an AA meeting. But I understand that at an AA meeting participants are encouraged to stand up and say, "I am Bob and I am an alcoholic." There is something incredibly healthy about this. There is an honesty and openness to this admission that can be transforming in a person's life. But it is not the only thing you want to say about Bob. Bob is not only an alcoholic. Bob is also a person in whom dwells the Spirit of the living God. Bob is vastly more than all the terrible things he has ever done during that part of his life when he was living as an alcoholic. The term "alcoholic" is not an adequate summary of the whole of Bob's identity.

We are destined for an identity much greater than the sad little things our small self has done in this life. We need to reflect upon our true identity. This is why it is valuable to look at Paul's list of the fruit of the Spirit. Here we will discover a description of our true self. Here we will find our real identity. We look at this list of fruit not in order that we might try to emulate these qualities. They are not qualities we are capable of manufacturing. We look at them as if they were a mirror showing us our true self.

When we examine the fruit of the Spirit, we discover who we truly are. We explore our authentic identity. The picture Paul gives of the fruit of the Spirit is a vision of our true human identity. It is an image of our high calling. Anything less than this fruit of the Spirit is something less than we are destined to be. We hold the list before us in order to keep our vision high, and to raise our sights to the fullness of all God intends us to be.

Living in the Freedom of the Spirit

Galatians 5:18

"The fruit of the Spirit" will be realized in our lives only as a result of our inner relationship with God. Paul says, "if you are led by the Spirit, you are not subject to the law." As we have seen in the previous chapter, to be "subject to the law" is to live in the "flesh," or according to our "lower nature." If we live "by the Spirit," on the other hand, Paul says we are no longer "subject to the law."

So what is wrong with being "subject to the law"? There are times when it might seem that it would be a good idea if we were all "subject to the law." Or more likely we might think it would be a good idea if other people were "subject to the law," especially if we were the ones to decide what those laws should be. It is tempting to place ourselves in the position of law-maker for the human community. But we might want to be cautious before establishing ourselves as the new Moses bringing down tablets from Mount Sinai.

The word Paul uses in Galatians 5:18 that is translated as "subject" is the Greek word *hupo*. It is a strong word. It is not a concept with which we want to trifle. *Hupo* means "power, rule, sovereignty, command." To be *hupo* to someone or something is to be under the authority of that person or thing. When we are *hupo* to someone, we bring ourselves into submission under that person.

It is tempting to think that it might be possible to run the world, or at least our own lives and the lives of those around us, by getting everyone to agree to be *hupo* to a simple, straightforward list of do's and don'ts. The Hebrew scriptures seem to support this idea of codifying behaviour in order to dictate human conduct according to a prescribed code. It has been estimated that the first five books of the Hebrew scriptures contain at least 613 commandments. These commandments cover everything from familial relationships to agricultural practices, personal grooming habits, and of course, issues of morality.

There is probably not a single person who is not in violation of several of these 613 commandments. Most of the men I know have cut their hair or shaved on occasion. And I know a few people who are hiding little tattoos under their clothing, and some who have loaned money at interest, and even a few who wear clothes made from a blend of textile materials, and perhaps even a few more who have eaten shrimp from time to time. All these actions represent violations of the Hebrew legal code.

One of the problems with such a code of human conduct is that over time circumstances change, and the circumstances that caused a law to make sense in one context may make the same law completely irrelevant in another situation. Laws written to accommodate the technological capabilities of three thousand years ago are not going to be able to accommodate eventualities that arise in the high-tech computer age in which we now live.

A fixed, written-down law is also inadequate because such a law cannot adjust to changes in awareness as the human family occasionally gains more enlightened understandings of the human condition. In Leviticus chapter 21, even a person with a slight physical disability is forbidden to serve as a priest in the conduct of the community's ritual worship. It is hard to imagine anyone today who would argue that physical disability should be a necessary barrier inhibiting full and free participation in all aspects of the human community.

It may be that few of us find ourselves tempted to make a complex and complicated list of rules to govern every possible human behaviour. There is, however, a deeper issue at stake in Paul's injunction that we are not "subject to the law."

Paul's contrast between being "subject to the law" and being "led by the Spirit" indicates a fundamental distinction in the way human beings orient their lives. It raises the question of who or what is really in charge of our lives. When we try to live "subject to the law," we are giving authority for our lives to something, or someone, out there. Whenever we find ourselves talking in terms of shoulds, oughts, and musts, we are attempting to live "subject to the law." We are running our lives according to an external standard of measurement.

While we may not give authority to the book of Leviticus in our lives, we probably have all found ourselves at times carrying around a kind of vision of what we think our lives ought to look like and attempting to conform to this vision. Or we have found ourselves worrying about what another person might think about our behaviour. How will this look? What would the people think of me if they knew what I am really like, or how I really feel about this? Most of us have adopted innumerable social norms and expectations that we carry inside our heads and by which we attempt to govern our lives.

The social norms we use to try to run our lives may come to us from our family, from the particular portion of society we value, or even from the church. It does not matter how we arrived at these values. If we attempt to govern our behaviour by any external norm, we are trying to live "subject to the law."

It seems that it was never God's intention that people look to the law as an external force or power to govern life. Speaking through the prophet Jeremiah, God says, "I will put my law within them, and I will write it on their hearts" (Jeremiah 31:33).

Even in the Hebrew scriptures God's goal seems to be that we should know God's presence dwelling in our innermost being and follow God's guidance in our own hearts. Ultimately we are not to govern our behaviour by any external means — not by law, not by social convention, not by the expectations of family members or friends. Throughout Christian history there have always been those who believed that God's inner guidance was calling them to live in opposition to the external guidance and direction of the whole of society. Many of these people have paid a high price for their determination to listen to the inner voice of God above the voice of society, religion, custom, or convention.

So strong is Jeremiah's conviction of God's direct inner guidance that he suggests we no longer need look to one another for teaching. "No longer shall they teach one another, or say to each other, 'Know the Lord,' for they shall all know me, from the least of them to the greatest, says the Lord" (Jeremiah 31:34). The teacher dwells within. Jesus says, "You know [the Spirit of truth], because he abides with you, and he will be in you" (John 14:17). This "Spirit of truth" is the teacher who will guide Jesus' followers after he has physically departed from them: "the Advocate, the Holy Spirit, whom the Father will send in my name, will teach you everything, and remind you of all that I have said to you" (John 14:26). The guidance we need is within.

It is fine to seek advice from another person. I consider it a privilege when someone comes to me seeking guidance. And I know that, without the consultation of others, I would have made many more stupid decisions than I have. But in the end we need to know that the truth we seek is within us. All another person can do is remind us of what we already know.

It is tempting at times for preachers to think their job is to come up with scintillating, entertaining new teaching. Preachers often fall prey to the idea that their job is to be entertainers, to keep the audience stimulated. The preacher, however, has a much less exalted calling. The preacher's job is simply to give voice to the truth that is already known deep within your own being. The preacher's job is to help each of us connect with that inner wellspring of wisdom and understanding that is the voice of God's Spirit residing in our heart. In good preaching we recognize the voice of truth that we have always known.

To live "by the Spirit" is to allow our lives to be governed and directed by the internal guidance of God's Holy Spirit. Paul says, "Where the Spirit of the Lord is, there is freedom" (2 Corinthians 3:17). Laws cannot set us free. Freedom comes only to those who have been set free by the Spirit, so that they are no longer controlled by external circumstance. Freedom means that we are able to live from a deep inner place of peace and balance. We are no longer yanked around in a reactive mode as the victim of whatever circumstances arise at a particular time.

In his letter to the Romans, Paul says that Christ has set us "free from the law of sin and death" (Romans 8:2). We are no longer in bondage. We are no longer under the law. In the opening verse of Galatians chapter five, Paul declares to his readers, "For freedom Christ has set us free. Stand firm, therefore, and do not submit again to a yoke of slavery" (Galatians 5:1). The freedom Christ gives us is not the freedom to do whatever we please. It is the freedom to find within ourselves the living presence of God and to live in accordance with the leading of God's Spirit.

No one can tell us exactly what being "led by the Spirit" is going to look like in our lives. Speaking of this Spirit who leads us, Jesus says, "The wind blows where it chooses, and you hear the sound of it, but you do now know where it comes from or where it goes. So it is with everyone who is born of the Spirit" (John 3:8). The Spirit of God cannot be locked up in a list of rules and regulations.

We are summoned by Christ to the extraordinary adventure of following where God leads. We are called to raise the sail of our own lives and allow the wind to direct our tiny sailboat. No one can say exactly what this will look like for you. We cannot predict how the wind of God's Spirit will flow in another person's life. We can only bear witness to one another through faithful adherence to the Spirit of God.

We can encourage one another to listen deeply to the Spirit who teaches and guides us. We can challenge one another to let go of those external demands, expectations, and requirements that so paralyse our lives. We can hold before one another the exalted vision of life lived in God's Spirit, as Paul describes when he tells us that those who live by the Spirit will find in their lives the qualities of "love, joy, peace, patience, kindness, generosity, faithfulness, gentleness, and self-control." Exactly how these fruits manifest in any person's life remains between that person and the God who is their guide.

The Grammar of Love

When we make a list of important items, there are two ways we might indicate which item is considered most significant. We might put the most important item first, or we might indicate its importance by placing it last. Paul uses both approaches. In his list of the fruit of the Spirit, Paul places the most important fruit first — "the fruit of the Spirit is love." In 1 Corinthians 13, Paul indicates the absolute primacy of love by placing it last. He says, "now faith, hope, and love abide, these three; and the greatest of these is love."

Whether it comes first, or last, there can be little doubt that, according to scripture and Christian tradition, love is the primary quality of the Christian life. The word *love* appears in a variety of forms in the Bible, at least 800 times. The words *hope, joy,* and *peace* each appear fewer than 300 times. When Jesus was challenged by the scribes to answer, "Which commandment is the first of all?" he replied, "You shall love" (Mark 12:30).

It is interesting, however, that apart from the gospel of John, Jesus barely spoke about love. In the gospel of Mark, the only time Jesus ever uses the word is when he quotes it in the summary of the law from Deuteronomy 6:4–5.

The absence of talk about love may point to the first and most important characteristic of love, as it is understood in the Christian faith. Love is something to be lived. It is not primarily something to be talked about.

Grammatically love can be either a noun or a verb. As a noun, love is something to acquire, something we look for, a quality or experience we hope to possess. We might spend a great deal of time and energy in search of love, believing that when we find it, our lives will make sense. When we find love, we hope that we will be happy and at peace with ourselves. We might advertise in the personal column of our local paper, "White single male seeking love," in the hope that this will bring the answer to our dreams.

Jesus seemed to think of love more as a verb than as a noun. Jesus said to his disciples, "I give you a new commandment, that you love one another. Just as I have loved you, you also should love one another" (John 13:34). If love can be commanded, then it is an action we can choose. We probably all learned from our earliest grammar training that a verb is an action word. This is only partly true. Not all verbs are action words. Some verbs describe states of being or existence. But when Jesus commanded his followers to "love one another," he was doing more than simply commanding them to be in a state of love. Jesus was directing his followers to love each other, he says, "Just as I have loved you." And Jesus demonstrated exactly what this love looks like by taking off his outer garment, tying a towel around his waist, pouring water into a basin, and washing his disciples' feet. Love, as Jesus lived it, is a foot-washing verb.

One Corinthians 13 is probably the most familiar chapter dealing with love in the Bible. But the most extended teaching on love is found in 1 John chapters 3 and 4. The writer of 1 John describes the true nature of love, saying, "Little children, let us love, not in word or speech, but in truth and action" (1 John 3:18).

Jesus did not describe love to his followers. He did not tell his followers what love should look like, or how to be more loving. Jesus simply loved and instructed his followers to do the same. He demonstrated, to all those he met, the qualities of life that he hoped to see born in their lives. Jesus understood that love is caught more than taught. If we follow Jesus' pattern, we will talk less about the things we believe and live our beliefs more fully.

The only hope we can have in using words is that our words might create an open space for us to connect with love. When we speak of love, we need to keep in mind that love is not a thing to be achieved. It is not a concept. We cannot define, dissect, analyze, categorize, or nail down what we are talking about when we talk about love. Love is connected with the concept of the human heart. The heart is that dimension of our being that is deeper than the mind, more profound than our thinking or our language. If we are going to know love, we must open to a deeper reality within ourselves.

One of the most definitive statements about love in the New Testament comes in the First Letter of John 4:16, where the writer says simply, "God is love." Now this is a most extraordinary thing to say. It is even more extraordinary if we turn it around. If it is true to say that "God is love," may it not also be true that in some sense "love is God"? Love is God's nature. Love is God's character. When we see love in action, we see God at work. Like love, God also is the ultimate Verb.

Love is the energy of the universe. Love is the dynamic life force that causes us to breathe, keeps our hearts beating, and urges blood through our veins. Love is the power that changes the seasons, causes the birds to migrate and the tulips to bloom after a long cold winter lying dormant in the ground. It is the creative spark that exists at the beginning of every human life. It is the motivation within human beings that enables us to live like God. Love is the force that causes human beings to create beauty. It urges us to extend ourselves in compassion and care to one another. Love is the source of all self-giving.

When we experience within ourselves the stirrings of gentleness, openness, and surrender, this is the action of love. And wherever love is moving, God is present, bringing meaning and purpose to human life. When we love, we are living in tune with our true nature. We are cooperating with our deepest created being. Without love we are something less than the extraordinary creatures we were created to be.

Paul says, "If I have prophetic powers, and understand all mysteries and all knowledge, and if I have all faith, so as to remove mountains, but do not have love, I am **nothing**" (1 Corinthians 13:2). Without love I am no-thing. I do not really exist. I do not really have life within me. Without love my life is an illusion. Love is reality. Anything that does not come from love is simply a fantasy.

People think they can satisfy their desires and longings by acquiring wealth, by shopping, or by fulfilling their greatest ambitions. Without love, none of these is anything. If we buy stuff without love, we simply accumulate clutter. If we live in a house without love, that house is not a home. It does not matter how much furniture we buy or how coordinated the paint colours are; without love, the house in which we live is just an empty shell. It may look like a home, but if there is no love in the house, it is not a home and the inhabitants are not really people.

Without love, the meaning and purpose of life are missing. It does not matter how pious we are, or how often we go to church. It does not matter if we know the Bible inside out, or if we can "speak in the tongues of mortals and of angels." If we "do not have love," we are only a "noisy gong or a clanging cymbal." Where there is no love, there is just empty sound. The grammar may be perfect, but the sentence has no meaning.

The writer of 1 John expresses this as strongly as he can, saying, "Whoever does not love does not know God, for God is love" (1 John 4:8). If we do not love, we do not know God. We may know **about** God, but without love it is something other than God we know. The writer of 1 John is not concerned about getting our theology right. He is concerned that we might truly and deeply know God. And God cannot be known by the mind. God is known only by love. The anonymous author of the fourteenth-century spiritual classic *The Cloud of Unknowing* says simply, God "may be well loved, but he may not be thought of. He may be reached and held close by means of love, but by means of thought never."[5]

In the gospels, the Pharisees knew all about God; they knew the scriptures and lived by the law. Jesus says of the Pharisees, "You tithe mint, dill, and cummin." They have observed the minute details of the law. But Jesus goes on to say, they have "neglected the weightier matters of the law." What are these "weightier matters? They are "justice and mercy and faith" (Matthew 23:23). They are all expressions of the presence and action of love. The Pharisees look good on the outside, but their insides are rotten because they have no love. Jesus says, "For you are like whitewashed tombs, which on the outside look beautiful, but inside they are full of the bones of the dead and of all kinds of filth" (Matthew 23:27).

This is a stinging rebuke and a sharp warning to anyone who lays claim to knowledge of God. Without "justice and mercy and faith," any knowledge of God we claim is a farce and a sham. The problem for the Pharisees is that they thought it was possible to know God simply by having ideas and information about God. But when the Bible speaks of knowing God, it means something far deeper and more intimate than merely knowledge in our minds. This deeper intimacy comes into existence only through love, never through mere thinking.

When we approach love, we encounter the extraordinary limitations of our thinking. We become aware of the inadequacy of information to convey a true awareness of the living presence of God.

---

5   Ira Progroff (trans.), *The Cloud Unknowing* (New York: Delta, 1957), p. 72.

The world does not want to know how much information Christians have, how profound our theology is, or how upright our morality. The world wants to see that we love. The world wants to see that we model ourselves after Jesus who came into the world because "God so loved the world that he gave his only Son, so that everyone who believes in him may not perish but may have eternal life" (John 3:16). Jesus is the manifestation in human history of the eternal nature of God that is love. To follow Jesus is to live according to the dictates of love and to bear God's love for all human beings with depth and honesty. As William Blake famously wrote, "We are put on earth a little space, / That we may learn to bear the beams of love."

We "bear the beams of love" by being like the source of love, the God in whose image we were created.

In 1 John 4:7, the writer says, "Beloved, let us love one another, because love is **from** God." This suggests that God sends love to us in order that we may be able to love. The King James version translates this verse saying, "Beloved, let us love one another: for love is **of** God." Love is of the very nature and character of God. When we love, we share in the being of God. Therefore the writer of 1 John goes on to make the extraordinary statement that "**everyone** who loves is born of God and knows God." This sounds outrageous, but it follows logically from what the writer has said about the nature of God. If in fact "God is love," then wherever we find love, we find something of God. Wherever we find people who love there is some knowledge of God.

Love is a universal human experience. There is nowhere God is absent. The psalmist asks God, "Where can I go from your Spirit? Or where can I flee from your presence?" And then the writer answers his own question, "If I ascend to heaven, you are there; if I make my bed in Sheol, you are there" (Psalm 139:7–8). There is nowhere that some shards of light cannot be seen, nowhere that love does not bear witness to the presence of the Creative Power at the source of all Creation.

Paul begins his list of the fruit of the Spirit with love because love is the beginning and the goal of all life. Love is the source of light, hope, and truth for all human beings. Love is the active Agent that brought all Creation into existence and sustains all life. As we receive the fruit of God's Spirit, we are drawn into the grammar of love and enabled to live in tune with the Verb who is love.

Taking Off the Outer Robe

Ⓣ here is a danger in describing love as primarily a verb. We may go on to describe the list of actions we believe characterize love and then mandate these actions for all people who want to be loving. When Jesus commanded his disciples to "love one another," he ran the risk of turning love into just one more law.

In John's gospel chapter 13 verse 34, Jesus gave the commandment to his disciples that they should love one another in the context of the symbolic action of foot washing. The love Jesus commanded was to be foot-washing love. Jesus never defined for his followers exactly what "foot-washing love" might look like in their own particular situation. We are each left to work out for ourselves the implications of what it might mean for us to wash one another's feet.

John's description of Jesus' foot washing action may however provide a key to the nature of this love commandment. John describes the scene, saying that

> Jesus, knowing that the Father had given all things into his hands, and that he had come from God and was going to God, got up from the table, took off his outer robe, and tied a towel around himself. Then he poured water into a basin and began to wash the disciples' feet (John 13:3–5).

There is a curious detail in this description. John says before washing his disciples' feet, Jesus "took off his outer robe." This action is the essential gesture of love. To take off our outer robe is to make ourselves vulnerable. It is to open ourselves, expose our tenderness. Taking off our outer robe means softening and opening to those around us. This action of opening and soften-ing is the essential nature of love.

It is so easy for us to face life with our outer robe firmly in place. We have our walls of protection so well built up. There seems to be no way to penetrate the exterior protective mecha-nisms we have constructed. We depend on these mechanisms to keep us safe. So we go out into the world with our guard up, always trying to read the signals, always trying to detect danger before the danger can get inside and hurt us.

You know what this feels like. It feels like the clenching in your stomach. It feels like the hardening and rigidity that sets in across your shoulder blades and down into your lower back. And you know the tone of voice this behaviour brings into your conversation. Your voice becomes a little bit clipped, the words come out faster than you meant them to, and they have a hard edge that you actually never intended. You probably say more than you really wish whenever you feel you have something to defend.

When our sense of well-being depends on keeping our de-fences up, we find more and more things to fear. Fear breeds fear. And the more we are afraid, the higher our walls become, the thicker our armour, and the more impenetrable the fortress we build around us. If you saw the movie *Panic Room*, you know that there are wealthy people who apparently build houses with completely self-contained steel rooms in the centre, where they can go and take refuge in the event of a burglary, a terrorist attack, or I suppose a nuclear strike from space. Most of us probably will not go to quite such lengths to preserve our sense of safety. But we may well have a panic room within ourselves, a dark little place where we go to hide whenever we feel insecure.

Jesus came to throw open the doors of our panic room. Jesus, taking off his outer robe, allowed himself to be made vulnerable. He faced danger without defensiveness, without hiding. This was not an easy thing to do. Jesus knew perfectly well that the people to whom he was making himself vulnerable could not be trusted. He knew they were going to let him down, betray him, and deny ever having known him. Jesus did not order Judas out of the room before taking off his outer robe. Jesus did not exclude Peter from his foot-washing love. He did not add a little moralistic sermon to his actions in order to make sure that the disciples would all know how bad they had been after their desertion. Jesus risked everything and served even those who were about to fail in the most spectacular fashion.

What made it possible for Jesus to take this extraordinarily bold step?

John the gospel writer says, "Jesus, knowing that the Father had given all things into his hands, and that he had come from God and was going to God, got up from the table, took off his outer robe," and prepared to wash his disciples' feet. Jesus was able to take off his outer robe, because Jesus knew "that the Father had given all things into his hands, and that he had come from God." Jesus knew who he was. He knew his true identity. He knew where he came from and where he was going. Jesus knew that there was something within himself that was stronger than all of the brokenness he was about to experience, stronger than his friends' failures, betrayals, and denials. Jesus trusted the light that was stronger than all darkness. He had experienced the fact that at the centre of his life was the living presence of God. Jesus rested and trusted in that strength. He had found a security that did not depend on external circumstances being a certain way.

Jesus did not need a physical panic room, because Jesus knew that within himself he had a stronger room than any steel or locks could ever provide. In one of the very few instructions about prayer Jesus ever gave his disciples, he said, "whenever you pray, go into your room and shut the door and pray to your Father who is in secret" (Matthew 6:6). The room here is the inner room of the human spirit. We are to go to this deep inner place within, and rest, and trust in God's presence. This is how we prepare for the action of love. This is how we find the strength and security to give up our braced attitude toward life.

When we discover that within us which is eternal, indestructible, and stronger than any of the external forces of life, then suddenly we are free. Suddenly we no longer need to protect ourselves. We no longer need to fight for our own little piece of the pie. We are liberated from the necessity to make ourselves safe. We know we are safe because, no matter what circumstances may arise, we are safe within.

We do not expect that the circumstances of our lives will always go the way we wish they would. But we know that, regardless of what may be happening on the surface of life, Jesus' final promise will always be true: "And remember, I am with you always, to the end of the age" (Matthew 28:20). Jesus promised his followers that, even when he was no longer physically available to them, they would always know his presence. They would always know that God's love dwelt in their innermost being.

When Jesus wanted to speak about this never-failing loving presence, he used the expression, "the kingdom of God." Most often Jesus used pictures or stories to describe this kingdom presence. Jesus asked his disciples, "What is the kingdom of God like? And to what should I compare it?" How do we experience God's loving presence in this world? How do we know this presence in our lives? How might we describe our awareness of God's presence? Jesus answers his own question, saying,

> It is like a mustard seed that someone took and sowed
> in the garden; it grew and became a tree, and the birds of
> the air made nests in its branches (Luke 13:18-19).

God's presence in the world, and in our lives, is like a seed sown in the ground that grows in the dark, innermost recesses of our being until it becomes a place of refuge, protection, and safety.

But there may be things about this seed image that we are not too comfortable with. Think about an apple in September.

The apple has been growing all through the summer, happily hanging from a branch high up in the tree. The apple sways in the wind and enjoys a beautiful view out over the orchard. It is content surrounded by other apples hanging nearby. There is a good sense of apple community in this tree and a great sense of security attached firmly to the strong branch of the tree.

Then one day, Apple notices that something terrible is beginning to happen. He realizes that, since the weather has cooled, one or two of his apple friends have gone missing. Then each day, a few more apples disappear. Terrified at this unsettling turn of events, Apple looks around for an explanation until finally one day he looks way down to the ground and sees his apple friends lying helplessly on the orchard floor below. Apple is terribly upset and cannot imagine what has happened.

Then one day he becomes aware that his own stem, which has held him securely attached to his own particular branch of the tree for his entire life is beginning to slip. He exerts all his energy and all his determination to hang on, but it is hopeless. One day, like his friends, Apple plummets to earth. He lands with an agonizing plop, bounces once, and then lies there bruised and dazed.

When Apple recovers from his fall he begins to notice that his beautiful, hard, shiny red skin is softening and that the flesh beneath the skin is getting squishy and juicy. Apple concentrates on keeping his exterior smooth and hard, but it is no use. Finally, one day a crack appears in his skin, juice oozes out, and Apple knows the end is near. There is nothing left he can do to preserve himself.

Now of course we know that, if Apple is going to fulfill his true destiny, he must fall from the tree. His external skin must break. The firm flesh beneath his skin must soften. Only as these things happen will the seeds in his core be released and fall into the ground. And only then will the extraordinary life force of these seeds be unlocked and the power of the apple be released to produce a magnificent new tree.

This life force that liberates a tree from a tiny seed has a name. Its name is love. It is the force and power of God. We must trust the reality of this power at the centre of our being. Jesus said, "Unless a grain of wheat falls into the earth and dies, it remains just a single grain; but if it dies, it bears much fruit" (John 12:24). To die is to let go of our securities, to soften and open, to surrender our determination to be in control of the forces of life. This is the death that leads to the fruit of God's Spirit being born in our lives, the death that connects us with the power of God at the centre of our beings and releases the force of life and love.

Like the apple, if we are to fulfill our destiny as human beings, we must acknowledge the presence of this indestructible force of love at the centre of our beings. We must be willing to fall from the tree. We must allow our exterior defences to be broken. We must take off our outer robe and soften toward life.

God's Surprising Welcome

There is a story from the ancient Christian desert tradition that illustrates profoundly the central nature of the Christian understanding of love.

> Two brothers went to market to sell the things they had made. When they reached the village, the brothers parted to sell their wares. As soon as they had separated, one of the brothers fell into fornication. When they met again, the first brother said, "My brother, let us return to our home." The brother who had fallen replied, "I am not going back." The other brother persisted saying, "My brother, why not?" The brother who had fallen said, "I cannot return to our community because as soon as you left me, I fell into fornication." The innocent brother, wishing to win over his fallen companion, said to him, "The same thing happened to me too, when you left me. Come, let us go and do strict penance and God will forgive us."
>
> Then the two brothers went to their elders and told them what had happened. The old men gave the brothers commandments for doing penance. So the innocent brother did penance for the other as though he had sinned himself. But God, seeing the affliction the innocent brother was giving himself for love's sake, made known to one of the elders that because of the great love of the brother who had not sinned, God had forgiven

the one who had sinned. See what it is to give one's soul for one's brother.[6]

Jesus summed up the law of love, saying, "You shall love your neighbour as **yourself**" (Matthew 22:39). This is commonly understood to mean that you should love your neighbour as much as yourself. Commentators have gone so far as to suggest that, in fact, we have two commandments here. Jesus is commanding us first to love ourselves in order that we might then be able to love others. This pop-psychology interpretation suggests that those who cannot love themselves will never be free to love others.

The alleged commandment to self-love, however, is found nowhere in the Christian scriptures. If we look at the example of Jesus' life and teaching, we see there is little evidence that Jesus ever recommended the path of self-love. Jesus recommended self-denial and death rather than self-love.

> If any want to become my followers, let them deny themselves and take up their cross and follow me. For those who want to save their life will lose it, and those who lose their life for my sake will find it (Matthew 16:24-25).

Jesus goes on to explain this statement, saying that "those who want to save their life will lose it, and those who lose their life for my sake will find it."

One of the only two other places in the gospels where the word "deny" appears is in the account of Peter's denial of Christ. In denying Christ, Peter was attempting to "save" his life. He was trying to protect himself. Like the apple hanging from the tree, Peter was struggling to hang on to his familiar position on the branch, assuming that his safety lay in clinging to his place. By clinging, Peter lost that to which he held. The key to love is not to grasp and hold on, but to let go of every external support, every

---

6   Based upon the story in *The Wisdom of the Desert*, 15:47.

external source of protection, safety, security, and identity. To deny myself is to let go of everything except God. It is in the transaction of surrender that true love for the neighbour is born.

When Jesus instructs us to "love your neighbour as yourself," he is not instructing us to love our neighbours as much as we love ourselves. He is instructing us to love our neighbour as if the neighbour is, in fact, our self. We are to see our neighbour not as other, not as separate, but as our self. We are to understand that we are united with all human beings. All division is broken down. We are united in the bond of love and fellowship with all people.

Paul says in Galatians, "There is no longer Jew or Greek, there is no longer slave or free, there is no longer male and female; for all of you are one in Christ Jesus" (Galatians 3:28). Clinging creates separation. Me and mine create division. We become aware of our deep oneness only when we lay down our own lives, surrendering those things that divide and separate.

Jesus is the primary demonstration of this love of the neighbour as the self. Jesus became human in order to manifest God's love for the world. The Christian understanding of the doctrine of the Incarnation teaches that, by being born in human form, Jesus became that which by nature he was not. Philippians says that Jesus, "though he was in the form of God, did not regard equality with God as something to be exploited, but emptied himself, taking the form of a slave, being born in human likeness" (Philippians 2:6–7). Jesus let go of that which was rightfully his in order to share in the limited condition of human nature.

Jesus chose to become human. He chose to identify fully with the human situation. He entered the mess of humanity in order to release the power of God's love in the world. Philippians 2:5 tells us to "let the same mind be in you that was in Christ Jesus." We are called to follow Jesus' example, becoming **the other** in order to manifest the depth and richness of God's love.

Any action that comes from an awareness of separateness

is less than the love to which Jesus calls us. When I perform an action from a position of superiority, as the good person performing a work of charity in order to do good to the other, my action will always diminish the other. An action is truly loving only when that action is done with the awareness that the other is not **other** at all. We are united in God's love in a common humanity and in the bond of Christ. What I do to the other, I do to myself and to Christ.

In the desert story above, the love of the second brother for his fallen companion was so great that he was willing to take upon himself his brother's sin. He was willing to be identified as his brother. He did not hold himself apart. He did not pretend that he was separate, that he was somehow different or superior. He joined his brother in the depth of his brother's fallenness and was willing to pay the price of his brother's sin, even though he himself was innocent. This desert story presents a vision of the true union at the centre of the Christian understanding of the human community.

Who is included in this vision? How wide are we willing to cast the net when we think of those with whom we are united?

Jesus appears to answer this question in the parable told in Matthew's gospel chapter 25 verses 31 to 46. A king gathers all the nations and divides them into sheep and goats. The division is decided on the basis of how the "nations" have treated those whom Jesus identifies as *"heni touton ton adelphon mou ton elakiston"* ("one of the least of these brothers of mine"). Commonly, the most pressing question in relation to this passage is seen to be the identity of "the least of these brothers." But more important is the question of who is being addressed in this judgement. Jesus says that "when the Son of Man comes in his glory," he will gather "all the **nations**." It is these "nations" who will be addressed in the judgement that is coming. So who are the nations who are separated into sheep and goats?

The word translated as "nations" in Matthew 25:32 is *ethnos*.

According to the J. B. Smith *Greek-English Concordance To The New Testament*, the word *ethnos* appears in the New Testament one hundred sixty-four times. Of these, *ethnos* is translated as "Gentiles" ninety-three times, as "nation" sixty-four times, as "heathen" five times, and simply as "people" twice. In the context of the New Testament, this means that the majority of occurrences of the word *ethnos* refer to "unbelievers."

It is never easy to figure out exactly when the translation "nation" is to be preferred. In almost all cases when the translation "nation" is chosen, the words "Gentiles" or "unbelievers" would make equal sense. At the end of Matthew's gospel, Jesus is reported to have instructed his disciples, "Go therefore and make disciples of all nations" (Matthew 28:19). It makes equal, and perhaps better sense, for Jesus to have said, "Go therefore and make disciples of all **unbelievers**."

In Matthew 24:9, the use of "unbelievers" to translate *ethnos* is probably to be preferred. If Jesus actually said, "You will be hated by all **nations**," he was wrong. "All nations" have not hated the followers of Christ. It surely makes more sense to understand that "**all unbelievers**" might hate the followers of Jesus. In Matthew 25:32, it is not immediately clear why the translation "nations" was chosen rather than "unbelievers." If we read Matthew 25:32 as saying, "All the unbelievers will be gathered," then Jesus is telling his disciples that the "unbelievers" will face judgement. It would be a comfort to those who were about to experience severe persecution at the hands of "unbelievers" to be assured that ultimately God's justice will be done. But the translation "unbeliever" in this context suggests an even more intriguing prospect for understanding this passage.

We know that the Christian church faced severe persecution in the first three hundred years of its history. It seems entirely plausible, however, that in the midst of this persecution there were occasions when Christians encountered kindness from those who were not believers. Just as there were non-Jewish people during the persecution of the Jews in Nazi Germany who protected Jews from their persecutors. So it seems plausible that there would have been non-Christian Romans who would have protected their Christian friends from the horrors of Roman persecution. What were the Christians to make of these loving, charitable, and kindly "unbelievers"? What were Jesus' followers to make of those people who treated them with kindness while the majority were treating them with violence and persecution?

What are we to make of the kindness and generosity of those who do not call themselves followers of Jesus and yet demonstrate by their actions the presence of love in their lives? The parable implies that these loving "unbelievers" are in fact following Jesus without really knowing it. Thus the "sheep's" question makes sense: "Lord, when was it that we saw you hungry and gave you food, or thirsty and gave you something to drink?" These "sheep" have served Jesus without recognizing that it was Jesus they served. The sheep's question would not make sense if asked by believers serving other believers. Christians serving other Christians would know that in serving one another they served Jesus. Surely they would recognize the presence of Christ in one another.

Jesus is saying here that Christ is present in the kindness and charity of unbelievers who serve others. In performing actions of grace and mercy, these "unbelievers" have, in fact, served Christ. They have responded to the prompting of love and have opened themselves to the presence of Christ in their lives without being aware that this is what they were doing. It is the presence of Christ, in love, that unites all humanity. We are bound together by the common bond of that which makes us most truly human, the presence of self-giving, sacrificial love.[7]

---

7   I am indebted to Brian Stoffregen for the intriguing possiblity that *ethnos* should be translated as *unbelievers* in the context. See http://www.crossmarks.com/brian/matt25x31.htm

Thomas Merton understood the inclusivity of this text and expressed it in the strongest terms.

> I must learn that my fellow man, just as he is, whether he is my friend or my enemy, my brother or a stranger from the other side of the world, whether he be wise or foolish, no matter what may be his limitations, "*is Christ.*" No qualification is needed about whether or not he may be in the state of grace. Jesus in the parable of the sheep and the goats did not stop to qualify, or say: "Whenever you did it to one of these My least Brethren, *if he was in the state of grace*, you did it to Me." Any prisoner, any starving man, any sick or dying man, any sinner, any man whatever, is to be regarded as Christ — this is the formal command of the Savior Himself.[8]

This parable points to the surprising nature of God's kingdom. It demonstrates that, at the final judgement, there will be those who are welcomed by God whom we might not have anticipated would find God's favour. There are those who have been secret followers of Jesus. Without knowing that it was Christ at work in their lives, there are people who open to the prompting of love in their hearts and, in doing so, are welcoming the presence of Christ, and responding to God's love.

---

8   Thomas Merton, *Disputed Questions* (New York: Harcourt Brace Jovanovich, 1960), p. 124.

The "Ever-Fixed Mark"

I cannot imagine that many musicians would have the audacity to compose a song with a five-line chorus made up of only five different words, one of which is repeated nineteen times. But 1967 was a year for pushing the boundaries and Paul McCartney and John Lennon were not just any ordinary musicians. So they wrote:

> All you need is love, all you need is love,
> All you need is love, love, love is all you need.
> Love, love, love, love, love, love, love, love, love.
> All you need is love, all you need is love,
> All you need is love, love, love is all you need.

It may not be the greatest poetry ever written. But it is hard not to applaud John and Paul's sentiment.

A slightly more profound statement about love was penned over four hundred years before Paul and John unleashed their poetry on the world. It was written by William Shakespeare, who in Sonnet 116 says,

> Let me not to the marriage of true minds
> Admit impediments. Love is not love
> Which alters when it alteration finds,
> Or bends with the remover to remove:
> O no! it is an ever-fixed mark
> That looks on tempests and is never shaken;
> It is the star to every wandering bark,
> Whose worth's unknown, although his height be taken.
> Love's not Time's fool, though rosy lips and cheeks

Within his bending sickle's compass come:
Love alters not with his brief hours and weeks,
But bears it out even to the edge of doom.
If this be error and upon me proved,
I never writ, nor no man ever loved.

Shakespeare identifies in this sonnet the fundamental Christian understanding of love. It is summed up in the apostle Paul's concise statement in 1 Corinthians 13:8, when he says simply, "Love never ends." Shakespeare expresses it somewhat more poetically, saying, "Love is not love / Which alters when it alteration finds."

Love is not affected by changing circumstances. Love "is an ever-fixed mark / That looks on tempests and is never shaken / It is the star to every wandering bark." Love is the constant guiding light for every ship lost at sea in the darkness and confusion of night. Love does not alter with the passing of time, but remains constant even to the point of death.

Love's not Time's fool, though rosy lips and cheeks
Within his bending sickle's compass come:
Love alters not with his brief hours and weeks,
But bears it out even to the edge of doom.

This love, which is constant and never-changing, is beyond human understanding. Shakespeare says, "It is the star to every wandering bark, / Whose worth's unknown, although his height be taken." Paul says, "For now we see in a mirror dimly, but then we will see face to face. Now I know only in part; then I will know fully, even as I have been fully known" (1 Corinthians 13:12). For both Paul and Shakespeare, love is surrounded on every side by a vast mystery pointing beyond itself to a reality greater than we can ever comprehend.

The mystery and wonder of this love have drawn human beings since the beginning of time, and have motivated people to reach beyond themselves in search of answers and understanding. This mystery drew a religious man named Nicodemus to approach Jesus in the hidden darkness of the night, seeking answers to the longings and questions of his heart.

Nicodemus was a Pharisee, "a leader of the Jews" (John 3:1). But his religion had not satisfied him. He knew there must be something more. He longed for understanding; he yearned to experience true life. When Nicodemus heard Jesus, the yearning inside him stirred. This preacher from Galilee ignited a light in Nicodemus's heart, and he was drawn to Jesus with his questions, even though this might cost him his reputation and position in society.

Jesus responded to Nicodemus by pointing him to the Source of love. Jesus taught that the answer could be found only by surrendering to the Source of love. Jesus said, "No one can enter the kingdom of God without being born of water and Spirit" (John 3:5). To be "born of water" is an image of baptism.

Baptism is the process of being stripped of everything that is not God. We go down into the water and die to this world. There is no external identity, possession, or experience in this life that we can take with us. In baptism we let go of everything that has ever defined us apart from God. And in this dying process we are born of the Spirit. We experience the living presence of God. We come to know God's presence, God's kingdom within our lives.

This is a mysterious process that no one can control. There is no way to make it happen. It cannot be programmed or predicted. Jesus says, "The wind blows where it chooses, and you hear the sound of it, but you do not know where it comes from or where it goes. So it is with everyone who is born of the Spirit" (John 3:8). The process of God's work in our lives is surrounded by mystery and wonder.

Nicodemus is puzzled by this teaching. He asks Jesus, "How can these things be?" (John 3:9). How indeed? It is often difficult to discover God's presence within the chaos of change and uncertainty. It seems so often that life is nothing but confusion and turmoil. In the words of the hymn that is often sung at funerals, "Change and decay in all around I see." How can we know "thou, who changest not"? What evidence is there of a love that "alters not with his brief hours and weeks, / But bears it out even to the edge of doom"?

In the face of change, uncertainty, confusion, and doubt, Jesus says, there is only one piece of evidence that will confirm in our hearts the reality of a love that "is never shaken." Jesus points to himself as the "star to every wandering bark." Jesus says, "God so loved the world that he gave his only Son, so that everyone who believes in him may not perish but may have eternal life" (John 3:16). Jesus is the evidence that the ultimate reality in life is not chaos, confusion, doubt, and darkness. In Jesus, God has demonstrated that the final irreducible fact of all existence is love: "God so loved the world." Despite all evidence to the contrary, love is reality. Love is true. Love is the "ever-fixed mark / That looks on tempests and is never shaken."

In an uncertain world, we long to find security and safety. Jesus teaches that the only way to find this strong secure place is to trust him: "God so loved the world that he gave his only Son, so that **everyone who believes** in him may not perish but may have eternal life." To believe in Jesus is to trust that what he says and demonstrates in his life is, in fact, true. To believe in Jesus is to trust that his picture of reality is the true picture and that the evidence of our senses is often less true.

This is why we need Jesus. The evidence of our senses so often seems to contradict the possibility that love is the true heart of the universe and the basis of all Creation. In Jesus, God has revealed the true nature of existence. When we trust in Jesus, we discover that hatred, anger, darkness, and despair are not the ultimate reality. When we trust Jesus, we discover within ourselves the reality of what Jesus calls "eternal life." Eternal life is not just life that goes on and on and on. Eternal life is a quality of life, present with us now, that is unshakeable, unchangeable, permanent, reliable, ever-faithful, and always true. To trust Jesus is to believe that there is, at the core of all existence, an unshakeable bedrock on which we can stand and which will never fail us, never let us down, and never betray us. This is the nature of love.

In John 3:16, Jesus describes what this love looks like. He says, "God so loved the world that he gave." The unshakeable love that is the Source of all being is a love that gives and gives and gives. All of life is a gift freely and graciously given. Our task is simply to open to that gift and receive all that has been poured out upon us.

Daniel Ladinksy's translation of the fourteenth-century Persian poet Hafiz asks the question,

How
did the rose
ever open its heart
and give to this world all of its beauty?

And the poet answers his own question, saying:

It felt the encouragement of light against its being,
otherwise we all remain too
frightened.[9]

We need to feel the "encouragement of light" against our being, and then, like the rose, we will open and give to the world all of our beauty. We will be able to follow the pattern of life that Jesus showed us, which is the true nature of God who "so loved the world that he gave." This giving is our true nature. But, as the poet points out, we are kept from this giving by fear.

---

9   Daniel Ladinksy (trans.), *Love Poems from God: Twelve Sacred Voices from the East and West* (New York: Penguin Compass, 2002), p. 161.

Giving requires that we open. Love is the opposite of fear and protection. It does not need to shelter itself. It does not need to hide. Love opens and pours forth from an abundance of life and energy. This is our true nature, which is reborn when we trust in Christ. This is what Jesus meant in John chapter three, when he told Nicodemus that he must be "born from above," or "born again."

To be "born again" is to return to our true nature, to be reconnected with that innocence and love in which we were originally created. To be "born again" is to become what we truly are, to reconnect with that which is unchanging and constant about us. It is to discover within ourselves that unchanging presence of love. When we are "born again," we come to know that we are that love that never "alters when it alteration finds." We have within ourselves that "ever-fixed mark / That looks on tempests and is never shaken." All these things in which we seek a sense of identity and security are passing away. They will all let us down. Only love remains.

The challenge of the Christian journey is to open to that quality of love, to renew our awareness of our true nature and to live in the strength, power, and permanence of the loving reality of God that is the source of all being. This is the "ever-fixed mark," "the star to every wandering bark."

When we rest and trust in this deep reality of love, we will not alter when we encounter unsettled circumstances. We will not bend according to the fickle whims of chance and change. When we rest in this love that is God, we will be free to live in tune with our true nature, revealed to us in Jesus. We will be "born again," and again, and again, as we continue to open to the light of God's presence and to receive the warmth of God's love shining in our being.

It takes sunshine to produce the fruit of our true nature. That sunshine has been provided and proved in the person of Jesus. The sunshine of God's love pours out on all those who turn toward it and allow it to open them and make them bloom.

The Joy
of Presence

$\mathcal{M}$ost of us have a confused picture of joy. What do you think of when you ponder the word *joy*? Many things might come to mind — the *Joy of Cooking*, the joy of the Lord, joy-ride, joy-stick, jumping for joy, "good tidings of great joy," "Joyful, joyful, we adore thee," "Joy to the world." The list could go on and on. Joy seems to pop up all over the place. But what is it we think we are really talking about when we use the word *joy*?

Roget's Thesaurus has quite a number of synonyms for the noun *joy*. They include: pleasure, thrill, kick, delight, gladness, exhilaration, happiness, well-being, blessedness, bliss, beatitude, gratification. At first glance, *joy* seems to be a feel-good kind of word. We hope to find joy, assuming that joy will make our lives more enjoyable.

All the dictionary definitions I have seen seem to identify joy with good feelings. And usually these good feelings we call joy seem to be connected with good circumstances occurring in our lives. When things are going well, we anticipate that we will find joy. When things are going badly, we assume that the outcome will be misery. The joy of cooking is somewhat diminished when we mistakenly put half a cup of salt into our cookie batter.

The New Testament appears to support this idea that joy is connected to favourable circumstances. In Matthew 2:10, when the magi in search of Jesus see that their guiding star has come to a halt, Matthew says, "they were overwhelmed with joy." Their long journey seems to be at an end. They anticipate a successful conclusion to their undertaking, and so they know a sense of well-being. They experience an intense feeling of contentment, peace, and harmony in their lives. The world is unfolding as it should, and the magi are "overwhelmed with joy."

Paul, writing in the epistles, frequently refers to "joy" in this way. In 2 Corinthians, Paul tells of having heard a positive report from Titus about the Christians in Corinth. In response to this encouraging news, Paul says, "In this we find comfort. In addition to our own consolation, we rejoiced still more at the joy of Titus, because his mind has been set at rest by all of you" (2 Corinthians 7:13). The idea of joy being connected to favourable circumstances is not particularly startling. We expect that, when things go well, we will feel good about life and, when things go badly, we will feel badly.

The problem with this picture, of course, is that circumstances are fickle. Even in the most charmed life, things do not always go perfectly all the time. There is a constant fluctuation in life. A situation that is wonderful one moment can turn into a nightmare the next. Even in seemingly trivial ways, a circumstance that made us feel good and positive can turn on us and dash our spirits.

I was heading out recently on a short trip with my wife. We had managed to pack and get ready with remarkable ease, peace, and harmony. The weather was perfect. We departed for our destination in lots of time, looking forward to a change of scene and a short break in our normal routine. I was driving along the highway happily talking with my wife about our lives and our plans for this trip.

The highway was not busy. We were cruising joyfully along without a care in the world when suddenly I noticed a man standing on the side of the highway waving a sign at me, indicating that I should pull over to the side of the road. He was a police officer. He informed me that I was exceeding the speed limit and he was going to issue me a speeding ticket. Suddenly, the joyful mood of setting off on a happily anticipated trip soured. The mood turned. We carried on our trip, driving more slowly and with a little less energy in our spirits.

Moods change. Feelings fluctuate. A joy that depends on circumstances being a certain way is a profoundly unstable thing. There are no states of being that remain consistent and unchanging. The state of joy can change in a moment. Aware of the fluctuating nature of circumstantial joy, the New Testament writers present a challenging perspective. In a number of passages it is possible to discern that they have a negative view of joy.

In Matthew chapter 13, Jesus tells the parable of the sower and the seed. The sower spreads seed abundantly and recklessly on all kinds of different soil. Some of the seeds "fell on rocky ground, where they did not have much soil, and they sprang up quickly, since they had no depth of soil" (Matthew 13:5). In the explanation that accompanies this parable, the seed that "fell on rocky ground" is said to describe people who hear "the word and immediately receive it with **joy**; yet such a person has no root, but endures only for a while, and when trouble or persecution arises on account of the word, that person immediately falls away" (Matthew 13:20–21). This kind of joy is superficial. It does not sink down into the depths of our being. It depends on good feelings, intensity, and hype.

Religion needs to be cautious about this "rocky ground" joy. It is lovely to gather together for powerful, stirring, and beautiful church services. Worship that feels moving can be a wonderful thing. When the choir sings like angels, the organ plays magnificently, and the preacher speaks with eloquence, it seems as if all is right with the world and God is truly in charge. Worship can be a source of great joy.

Relationships can also be a source of joy in the church. The fellowship within the community of faith can often be warm, meaningful, and comforting. There are times when the intimacy and support of the Christian community sustain and strengthen us with love, compassion, and deep care. Like worship, the community of faith has the potential to bring great joy into the lives of those who commit themselves to this community.

But worship and community can also be a source of deep pain and extraordinary anguish. What happens to our joy when the choir sings out of key? What happens to our joy when the choir leader becomes abusive and belligerent to those choristers who do not measure up to the standard of musical excellence that has become the norm? What happens to our joy in community when those we have come to depend on fail us? What happens when the community that was once a source of joy turns and becomes a source of pain and anguish?

If we are to know true joy, our joy must come from a source deeper than circumstances. The biblical vision of joy is based on the conviction that there is a dimension within every human being that is unchanged by the constant fluctuations of unstable circumstances. True joy does not depend on things going well or people being nice. True joy lies hidden in the inner depths of our being and is found when we come to recognize that there is that within us which is rooted in the unchangeable, eternal, faithful presence of God.

When Jesus was speaking about the presence of God, he used the expression "kingdom of heaven." The "kingdom of heaven" is that dimension of reality in which God's presence is known and honoured. Jesus used the picture of a hidden treasure to speak about God's presence: "The kingdom of heaven is like treasure hidden in a field, which someone found and hid; then in his joy he goes and sells all that he has and buys that field" (Matthew 13:44). There is a treasure hidden deep within our being that is worth everything we are and all that we possess. This hidden treasure is the source of joy.

We are like people who walk around all day with a cheque in our pockets for a million dollars. And yet we spend our lives worrying about how we are going to pay our credit card bill. We need to reach down deep within ourselves and encounter the living reality that is the true source of joy.

The Greek word for joy is *chara*. In its root, *chara* is closely connected to the word *charis*, which means "grace." So "joy" in the New Testament is closely associated with the idea of gratitude. In her poem "Wage Peace," the poet Judyth Hill advises us that, in order to discover peace in the world, we might "learn the word thank you in three languages." This is good advice for "joy" as well. Joy is the companion of thank you.

We will experience joy when we recognize how gifted we are. When we sift through the fluctuating circumstances of our lives with gratitude, we will find that joy rises up within our hearts. Joy comes from acknowledging that, no matter how challenging our circumstances may be, we have been blessed. Life is a gift. This world in which we are privileged to live is a gift. The people in our lives, even the ones who seem intent on destroying our joy, are all gifts given by God.

It may not always feel that way. But this is not about feelings. This is about reality. And the reality is that we have been gifted. We are blessed people. The ability to breathe is a gift. We do not make our breath happen. We do not keep our hearts beating. These functions of life are given to us by the Source of life, in whom is found true joy that cannot be taken from us.

When I received my speeding ticket, as I headed out on a trip with my wife, I could have viewed it as a curse or a blessing. I chose eventually to see that little blue slip of paper as a blessing. It reminds me that I have driven safely for thirty years. It reminds me that driving is a profound spiritual discipline. When I rush, I put myself in danger. When I fail to pay attention to what is going on around me, or to my own actions, I put myself, and others, in jeopardy.

The speeding ticket I received reminds me to slow down, to stay conscious, to remember that I live in a world inhabited by other beings as well as myself, and that my actions have consequences for those other beings as well as myself. I can give thanks for the police officer whose conscientious performance of his duty helped to wake me up and caused me to pay more careful attention.

When I say thank you, I am opening myself to a deeper dimension of life, a hidden purpose and reality that exists at the heart of everything. I am acknowledging that there is a Gift Giver. I am opening myself to the Presence of the Gift Giver in every event of my life. The awareness of God's Presence in every circumstance is the meaning and the Source of Christian joy.

The Dimension of Peace

Of all nine fruit of the Holy Spirit listed by Paul in Galatians 5:22, peace may well be the most universally desired and the most consistently elusive.

Human beings seem to find it impossible to live in peace. Nation goes to war against nation, families feud among themselves, and individuals experience turmoil and unrest within. Why is it so difficult for people to find and maintain peace?

The first thing to observe about peace is the fundamental spiritual principle that you cannot give that which you do not have. Jesus said, "Peace I leave with you; **my** peace I give to you" (John 14:27). Jesus was able to give peace to others because he had peace himself. I cannot give you a million dollars because I do not have the money. I can promise you all I want that one day I will give you a million dollars. But the likelihood of my ever possessing such money is profoundly remote. And what I never have, I can never give. I can make promises. I can exert enormous effort to fulfill my promises; but I cannot give what I do not possess. If we want to give peace to others, we must have peace within ourselves.

Why is peace so often lacking within our lives? Why is life so often characterized by turmoil, unrest, disharmony, and unhappiness?

Paul helps us understand why peace is such an elusive quality when he writes in Romans, "To set the mind on the flesh is death, but to set the mind on the Spirit is life and peace" (Romans 8:6). Paul presents for us here two distinct ways of living: one he calls setting "the mind on the flesh," the other he calls setting "the mind on the Spirit." It is important to understand what Paul means by these two phrases.

When Paul talks about setting "the mind on the flesh" he is talking about a specific perspective on life and, particularly, on the human condition. He is talking about a particular way of looking at life.

For Paul, to "set the mind on the flesh" is to fall prey to the illusion that material reality is all there is to life. To "set the mind on the flesh" is to view human beings as nothing more than physical, biological entities, little machines occupying space on earth for a short time and then one day disappearing. In Paul's understanding, when we take this view of the human condition, we will naturally spend our lives focused primarily on our physical circumstances. To "set the mind on the flesh" is to believe that human existence is defined entirely by physical reality, and that the meaning of life is found in orchestrating our external circumstances so that things run the way we want them to run.

When I "set my mind on the flesh," I define personal worth in terms of measurable achievement and success. I place my sense of personal need, want, and desire ahead of any other consideration. When I "set my mind on the flesh," I am saying that I am the centre of my universe. I am interested primarily in my agenda. My comfort, my well-being, my own individual sense of how things should be, are the primary considerations in my life. I am saying that I want things my way. I want life to dance to the tune that I play. When I "set my mind on the flesh," I view you as existing only to make me feel better, to help me get along in life and to fulfill my vision for the world. I am concerned only with my feelings, my longings, my hopes and aspirations.

When I "set the mind on the flesh," I view any opposition to my will as an enemy to be destroyed. Anything that gets in my way is simply an obstacle to be crushed, so that the path as I require it can be smoothed out ahead of me. People who have "set the mind on the flesh" build walls of protection and insulation around themselves. They do not give; they can only take and protect. They live in fear that someone is going to take something from them. They are convinced that there is not really enough to go around, and therefore they must hold on with all their might to the meagre pittance life has given them.

It is easy to see why a world full of people who have "set the mind on the flesh" might be a world in which it is difficult to find much peace. Paul calls it a world of "death." This is not an exaggeration. When I have "set the mind on the flesh," I do not have true life within me. Jesus asked his disciples, "Is not life **more than** food, and the body **more than** clothing?" (Matthew 6:25b).

When my first concern is with my physical circumstances, I have lost touch with this "more than" quality of life. I have fallen prey to the illusion that the meaning of human existence can be summed up by the things I own, the things I do, and the impression I make in the world. This is not life. When I make the mistake of believing that my external circumstances are life, I bring death with me wherever I go. I destroy life. I cut off that which is most true and most real about my humanity.

The problem is that we think peace will be found by looking after ourselves in "the flesh." We think peace comes from getting our way. We believe that peace will be established when we build a big enough wall around ourselves so that no one can get in to hurt us. We think peace is found in being the biggest, strongest, richest, most successful person on earth. But there is no peace in the realm of the flesh. There will never be peace if peace depends on getting circumstances to turn out a certain way.

Just before his crucifixion, as he was entering Jerusalem for the last time, Jesus looked down on the city and, Luke says, "he wept over it, saying, 'If you, even you, had only recognized on this day the things that make for peace!' " (Luke 19:41–42). What are "the things that make for peace"? Jesus goes on to answer this question in a rather obscure but nonetheless forceful way. Expanding upon his lament over Jerusalem, Jesus says,

> Indeed, the days will come upon you, when your enemies will set up ramparts around you and surround you, and hem you in on every side. They will crush you to the ground, you and your children within you, and they will not leave within you one stone upon another; because you did not recognize the time of your visitation from God (Luke 19:43-44).

Jesus is challenging the people of Jerusalem to recognize that everything they cherish, everything they cling to, is going to be taken from them. Everything they were unable or unwilling to surrender, they are going to lose. They are going to lose everything because they failed to recognize God's presence in their lives: "You did not recognize the time of your visitation from God." When we recognize "the time of our visitation from God," no one can take anything from us that we cannot readily surrender. There is nothing left to defend. When there is nothing left to defend, we discover God's peace.

It all hinges on recognizing "the time of your visitation from God." In Jesus Christ, God has come. God has visited the human situation and dwells for all eternity with those who are willing to acknowledge the presence of God. This is why, at the announcement of Jesus' birth, the angels sang, "Glory to God in the highest heaven, and on earth peace among those whom he favours!" (Luke 2:14).

Jesus is the Prince of Peace. Jesus is the source of inner healing and life given to all people who will open to the awareness of his presence. Jesus is the power of love and light shining in the world. Jesus is the final proof that life is "more than food, and the body more than clothing."

There are two things that "lead to peace" — waking up and letting go. When we recognize God's "visitation" and, in response, surrender everything to the God who has come to us, then our feet are set upon the path to peace.

Paul says that instead of living with the mind set "on the flesh," we should "set the mind on the Spirit." To "set the mind on the Spirit" is to understand now that life is "more than food, and the body more than clothing." It is in this "more than" dimension that peace resides. In this "more than" dimension of life we know that God has come, and that God alone is the source of life and peace for all people.

Religion is often called "a crutch." Well, a person with an injured leg is no fool when he uses a crutch. The efforts we make to live without the support of a life force and a truth greater than ourselves bring violence, destruction, and death into the world. The cold, hard evidence of history demonstrates that by ourselves, we human beings do not know how to live together in peace and harmony. We do not know how to build the kingdom of light and truth for which our hearts long. We do not even know how to live at peace with ourselves.

It only makes sense to look beyond ourselves and ask ourselves if there might not be a force and a power that can enable us to discover that peace for which we long. Is there not an alternative to the grasping, demanding, self-centred obsessions that characterize so much of what passes for human life?

Paul says there is another way. We need to find a different centre within ourselves that will guide our lives and nourish us with truth and grace. We need to put aside self-interest, self-protection, and fear. We need to open to the gentle guidance of God's Holy Spirit. We need to recognize the strong tenderness and softness that form our true nature. We need to acknowledge our need for the strong wisdom and support that reside in a power greater than ourselves. This is the only path to peace. This is the only hope for the human community to find new ways of living together in harmony and peace.

Go to that place within yourself where you can recognize that the "visitation" of the Lord has come. Acknowledge the presence of God at the heart of your being. Never forget that there is a deeper dimension to life that makes us who we truly are. Resist the temptation to remain trapped on the surface of life, caught up in daily circumstance.

Go into the depths of your being. Discover within yourself the Source of all peace who resides within you. Acknowledge the Prince of Peace who gives you the gift of life and continues to sustain, strengthen, and guide you throughout all your days.

The Path of Patience

Let me begin my discussion of patience with a disclaimer I have often had occasion to use. It comes from Wendell Berry, who said in his wonderful poem, "A Warning to My Readers":

> Do not think me gentle
> because I speak in praise
> of gentleness, or elegant
> because I honor the grace
> that keeps this world.

So I say, do not think me patient because "I speak in praise of" patience. And, to continue with Berry's poem,

> I am a man crude as any,
> gross of speech, intolerant,
> stubborn, angry, full
> of fits and furies.

Patience is not my automatic first response in many situations.

Patience is a most difficult virtue. We live in an extraordinarily hurried society. We look for instant gratification and are seldom comfortable waiting for anything. The "Canadian Newswire, 5 January 2005" reports that "Canadian household debt balance has increased by 18 per cent from $56,700 in 1999 to $66,900 in 2003."[10] Even without being good with numbers, I know that this means a lot of people owe a lot of money.

---

10 http://www.newswire.ca/en/releases/archive/December2003/10/c1295.html

I have no doubt that some of this debt is unavoidable. But I also know that much debt has accrued because we want what we want, and we want it now. We would rather not wait until our bank accounts are adequate to support the kind of lifestyle we think we deserve. We are not a naturally patient culture. And the lack of patience has certain unfortunate consequences in our lives.

I imagine that most of us would agree that patience, for the most part, is a desirable but difficult quality. So what is this patience that we desire but find it hard to experience in our lives?

The Greek word Paul uses for patience in his list of the fruit of the Spirit is a curious word. He uses the word *makrothumia*. It is actually a single word made up of two separate words: the word *makro* and the word *thumeo*. *Makro* means long, and *thumeo* means anger. So literally, the word *makrothumia*, which is translated as "patience," means "long anger." It does not sound much like a virtue toward which we might be encouraged to strive. It is interesting that Paul uses this same word *makrothumia* in another context in which he directly connects it with anger.

In Romans 9:22, which is a truly difficult verse, Paul asks, "What if God, desiring to show his wrath and to make known his power, has endured with much *makrothumia* the objects of wrath that are made for destruction?" Leaving aside all the challenging aspects of this hypothetical question, Paul seems at least to be suggesting that, although God might have destroyed those who merit anger for their behaviour, instead God has held back in order that, as Paul goes on to say, God's merciful character might be made known. So the implication in this context is that *makrothumia* is anger delayed.

Long anger is slow anger. We are familiar with the idea of being "short-tempered," and know the disastrous consequences that usually follow from short-tempered actions and choices. To be *makrothumia* is to be long-tempered. It does not mean repressing or pushing down our anger. It means, rather, taking a step back from our initial response to a difficult situation. To be *makrothumia* is to take a breathing space before responding to whatever stimulation has come into our life. *Makrothumia* is anger that does not vent itself right away. It holds back. It waits. It is patient with the situation that is causing the feeling of anger in order that something more true than the anger, and more real than the irritating situation, might be able to emerge.

There is a natural connection between anger and patience. We usually lack patience because we are angry. And we usually show anger because we lack patience. In a sense, even when we are impatient for something good, we could say that we are angry with the delay of whatever good thing it is for which we are waiting impatiently. So to be patient is to choose not to respond to a particular set of circumstances with anger. To be patient is to allow circumstances that may not be to our liking, to simply be, as they are.

The great New Testament vision of patience comes in James's letter chapter five, where the writer exhorts his audience to

> Be **patient**, therefore, beloved, until the coming of the Lord. The farmer waits for the precious crop from the earth, being **patient** with it until it receives the early and the late rains. You also must be **patient**. Strengthen your hearts, for the coming of the Lord is near. Beloved, do not grumble against one another, so that you may not be judged. See, the Judge is standing at the doors! As an example of suffering and **patience**, beloved, take the prophets who spoke in the name of the Lord (James 5:7–10).

I spent seven years in Manitoba. For five-and-a-half of those years I lived in a small farming community an hour's drive west of Winnipeg. I have a lot of sympathy for farmers. Farming is a wonderful life — when it works. But farming is enormously challenging. Farmers are at the whim of forces of nature, economy, and time that are far beyond their ability to control. We all share this lack of control in common with farmers. But farmers, of necessity, are more conscious of their helplessness before external forces over which they have no power. So farmers are constantly challenged to look at how they respond when life is not unfolding as they think it should.

When things are not going well for a farmer, it is no doubt tempting to curse fate and respond with anger, to rail against all those forces that seem to be conspiring against you, making your life impossible. Standing out in your field, shaking your fist at the wind that is ravaging your topsoil, is a foolish waste of energy. Even anger at the local bank, which is foreclosing on your mortgage, will accomplish nothing. Anger will never change the weather and is unlikely to convince the bank. So farmers are in the particularly blessed position of having to learn to respond to life without the luxury of a fiery temper. They must acquire patience that is slow anger.

James gives exactly this advice earlier in his letter in chapter one, where he instructs his reader, "You must understand this, my beloved: let everyone be quick to listen, slow to speak, slow to anger; for your anger does not produce God's righteousness." We become angry when we feel our lives are out of control. It is painful to experience our lives as being out of control. And most of us do not like pain.

In the King James Version of the Bible, the Greek word *makrothumia* is translated as "longsuffering." When we are angry, we are trying to avoid the pain of recognizing the truth about our lives — that our control over the forces of life is an illusion. None of us is in control of the circumstances of our lives, and we need to get used to this reality and stop fighting against it. When I am impatient, it is because I do not want to experience pain any longer.

Consumer debt is driven in part by our culture's desire to avoid pain. Shopping is a form of anaesthetizing ourselves against the pain of unfulfilled expectations and desires. We shop to reward ourselves for putting up with the drudgery of life. We shop to escape, for a moment, from the pain of living with life as it presents itself. To be patient is to accept that life does not always meet our desires, expectations, even our basic needs, and to discover that we can live with this fact.

Patience opens us to the realization that there are better ways of finding fulfillment in life than getting an occasional adrenalin high from some new purchase or from wrestling the circumstances of our lives under our control. The writer of Hebrews says,

> And we want each one of you to show the same diligence so as to realize the full assurance of hope to the very end, so that you may not become sluggish, but imitators of those who through faith and **patience** inherit the promises (Hebrews 6:11–12).

It is "patience" that enables us to "inherit the promises." The promises the writer goes on to spell out affirm that we will discover a "refuge," and that we will be "encouraged" and will "have this hope, a sure and steadfast anchor of the soul" (Hebrews 6:18–19). When we find ourselves confronted with circumstances that make us angry, what we are really longing for is a place of rest. We are looking for a place of strength and security. This place is not a temple built by human hands. This place of encouragement cannot be purchased in a mall or harvested from a field. It dwells within "the inner shrine behind the curtain" (Hebrews 6:19).

To be patient is to rest in this inner sanctuary of our being where "Jesus, a forerunner on our behalf, has entered" (Hebrews 6:20). To be patient is to be where Jesus is. Jesus does not need to resort to anger and resentment. Jesus has shown the way forward, past all suffering, turmoil, and unrest. The way of patience lies through the cross of Christ, in which we join Jesus and surrender our need for control. We give up our determination that things should be other than they are, and we accept the circumstances of our lives just as they are.

Patience understands that we are powerless in the face of most of the forces of life. Jesus challenged his disciples, asking them, "can any of you by worrying add a single hour to your span of life?" (Matthew 6:27). We are not the masters of the universe. We are not in charge of our ultimate destiny as human beings. When we give in to anger and impatience, we are like a farmer standing in his field, shaking his fist at the rain that is drowning his crops. When we are patient, we accept the realities of life as they present themselves and we do not rail against the difficulties we encounter.

Nor, however, do we look at the difficulties of life and simply resign from the struggle. Patience recognizes that the only healthy, life-giving place from which to begin to address the realities of life is from a place in which we acknowledge and accept our circumstances as they are. Patience says, "This is where I am," and opens to the realities of life as they are. Patience is then able to move forward with a more steady, balanced, sane perspective to deal with life as it is.

Patience sees the bigger picture, knowing that the present difficult circumstances will eventually change. If we fight against our circumstances and force them to change, we will miss the lesson that our present situation has to teach us. The circumstances of our lives as they are have the power to shape our lives and conform us more fully to the image of God in which we have been created.

As James pointed out, "anger does not produce God's righteousness." Anger does not bring us into line with God's will. Anger does not lead to right action or healthy choices. The path of "righteousness" lies along the way of patience, which is the way of surrender. Patience enables us to connect with a new resource within ourselves that is the living presence of God known to us in Christ.

Being the Kindness You Are

In discussing patience, I suggested that the Greek word *makrothumia* refers to anger that is delayed, that does not vent itself right away. This does not mean repressing our anger, or even pretending it is not there. True patience acknowledges that the situation in which we find ourselves is not one that we might have chosen for ourselves. It acknowledges the difficulty and pain we experience, and even the irritation, frustration, and anger. But then patience chooses to respond without giving free reign to our feelings.

Patience is a kind of buffer zone we build between stimulus and response. To be patient is to create space between whatever it is that causes us to feel we need to react and the moment in which we actually choose to respond.

The purpose of creating this breathing space between stimulus and response is to allow something other than our initial reaction to emerge. Patience allows us to respond to a situation rather than simply reacting with an automatic knee-jerk instinct. Our first conditioned reaction might not be the best way of responding in certain situations. The conviction is that, if we give ourselves space and time, something better will emerge than might at first arise in the heat of the moment.

One of those better things that will emerge, if we practise patience, is the next fruit of the Spirit. If we step back from our irritation and give ourselves space, we will discover that kindness bubbles to the surface.

One of the things I love most about Paul's list of the fruit of the Spirit is how ordinary they are. They are not splashy and loud. Manifesting the fruit of the Spirit will probably never make you rich, powerful, or famous. The fruit of the Spirit are simply solid, good qualities found in God and given to human beings by virtue of the presence of God's Spirit in our lives.

Nowhere is this unspectacular nature of the fruit of the Spirit more evident than with the fruit that Paul calls "kindness." It does not take any special talent to be kind. You do not have to be smarter than anyone else. Kindness is a simple, positive, life-affirming way of responding to the world around us. It is not complicated or bewildering. If we are willing to listen to the Spirit speaking within ourselves, we will always have a sense of what the kind response would be.

However, the fact that we might know what the kind response is in any situation does not mean that the kind response is always easy. Kindness is enormously challenging.

Jesus uses the adjective "kind" in Luke's gospel, chapter 6 verse 35, to describe the nature of God. Leading up to this passage Jesus has been giving his followers some of the most difficult instructions in his entire teaching, saying,

> Love your enemies, do good to those who hate you, bless those who curse you, pray for those who abuse you. If anyone strikes you on the cheek, offer the other also; and from anyone who takes away your coat do not withhold even your shirt. Give to everyone who begs from you; and if anyone takes away your goods, do not ask for them again (Luke 6:27–30).

If you do not think that these are difficult instructions to follow, you are a better person than I am. I do not want to love my enemies. And I certainly do not want to do good to those who hate me. I want to stand up for my rights and make sure that I am not trampled on.

My daughter came home from the store recently, having attempted to return a broken item a week after she had purchased it. She had the receipt and the original bag from the store. An exactly identical item was on the shelf in the store, so the exchange could easily have been made. The cashier was about to exchange the item when the manager came by and asked what was going on. When the manager was informed about this perfectly routine transaction, he became abrupt and said, "Well, what am I supposed to do with the one you are bringing back? I can't sell it again. Get it fixed and send me the bill for the repair."

When I heard this story, I was determined to phone the manager and express my outrage that my daughter should be treated in such a shabby manner. And Jesus looked at me and said, "If anyone takes away your goods, do not ask for them again." "But that is not right," I replied. "It's not fair. Why should I allow my daughter to be treated with such disrespect? That manager should not get away with such behaviour." And Jesus paused for a while and said, "Pray for those who abuse you." "But why?" I wailed.

And this is just the question Jesus wants me to ask: "Why should I be kind to the obnoxious store manager?" The answer to this question is found in my true destiny. I was created in the image of God. My destiny is to live in such a way that the image of God is being restored in my life. When I respond out of my first reaction of outrage, I am choosing to live as something less than I was created to be. Jesus wants to enable me to live more like the extraordinarily exalted being that is my true nature. My destiny is to become more like God in whose image I was created.

So what is God like? Well, Jesus replies, that is another very good question. And the answer follows quite quickly in Luke 6:35–36, where Jesus says,

> But love your enemies, do good, and lend, expecting nothing in return. Your reward will be great, and you will be children of the Most High; for he is kind to the ungrateful and the wicked. Be merciful, just as your Father is merciful (Luke 6:35–36).

God is kind, not just to those who deserve kindness. God is kind, not only to those who are polite all the time, who never upset me or let me down. God is kind to those who are "ungrateful." And God is kind even to those who are "wicked."

Who are these "ungrateful" and "wicked" that Jesus speaks about? It would be me. I am the "ungrateful." I am the "wicked."

Think about the world we live in. We live here, in what is called the "Western world," in incredible luxury, privilege, and comfort. As Rex Murphy says, "Those of us born in this part of the world have already won the only lottery that really counts." Around the corner of the globe in Asia 200,000 people had their lives swept away by a massive tsunami wave. The suffering inflicted on the people of Indonesia, Sri Lanka, India, Thailand, Somalia, Myanmar, Maldives, Malaysia, Tanzania, Bangladesh, Kenya, and the Seychelles on 26 December 2004 is utterly horrifying. It is hard to imagine 200,000 deaths in one day. It is hard to comprehend the destruction in those countries.

But suffering and devastation did not begin in our world on 26 December 2004. In South Africa 700 people a week die as a result of HIV/AIDS. In Niger, Sierra Leone, Afghanistan, Malawi, Guinea and Liberia, Guinea-Bissau, and Somalia, the child mortality rate is more than 200 deaths per 1,000 births. These death rates are a result of HIV/AIDS, starvation, poor water supply, and lack of adequate medical care.[11]

According to the United Nations, every day in our world 24,000 people die as a result of starvation. This means that every week as many people die of starvation in our world as died in the terrible tsunami that hit South Asia at the end of 2004.

And yet, here I am getting twisted out of shape about the possibility that someone has not been polite to my daughter. A person like me deserves God's wrath and anger. A person like me

---

11 http://www.who.int/inf-pr-2000/en/pr2000-67.html

who goes to bed well fed and comfortable every night of my life in a world where many live in utter destitution, and yet complains about my little inconveniences, deserves to be punished. And yet, God treats me not with the punishment I deserve, but with kindness and mercy. God does not deal with me according to my ingratitude and insensitivity. In the very midst of my wickedness, God treats me with grace, mercy, and gentle kindness.

The point here is not to beat myself up and take on responsibility for all the pain and suffering of the world. The point is to allow the suffering I see in the world around me to encourage me to respond with greater kindness in every circumstance. Jesus says, "Be merciful, just as your Father is merciful" (Luke 6:36). If I want to be like God, I am going to have to learn to respond with kindness to the store manager who treats my child without adequate respect.

If I want to fulfill my true destiny as a being created in God's image, I am going to have to respond with kindness to the person who fails to fulfill my expectations for their life. I am going to need to respond over and over with kindness to those who have hurt me again and again, and who it is so hard for me to forgive.

But the miracle of kindness is that, the more kind I am, the more kindness grows. The more I am able to respond with mercy where I am, the more I will understand what it means for me to be merciful in response to a world of great suffering and pain. The more I practise kindness where I am, the more I will be empowered to respond with true kindness in whatever situation confronts me.

One of the foundational gospel principles that relates to the fruit of the Spirit is that, the more we use what we have been given, the more what we have been given will grow. In the parable of the talents in Matthew 25, Jesus shows that what we use grows and bears more fruit in our lives; what we bury dies. Jesus sums up this teaching by saying, "For to all those who have, more will be given, and they will have an abundance; but from those who have nothing, even what they have will be taken away" (Matthew 25:29). If we do not use it, we will lose it. Kindness breeds kindness in our own lives and in the lives of those around us.

I cannot assume personal responsibility for world hunger or for the terrible infant mortality rates that afflict so much of our world. I cannot solve the horror of the HIV/AIDS epidemic. I cannot fix the silent hidden pain that I know is present in the lives of so many people all around me. But I can be more kind to the people I live with, to the people I run up against who irritate me. I can be more kind to the people with whom I disagree, or who upset me or cause me to feel uncomfortable. And the kinder I am where I am, the more kind I will become. And the more kind I become, the more kindness there will be in the world.

But do not turn this into another make-work project. I cannot create kindness. We are talking here about "fruit." God is the source of kindness. There is kindness in me because God is in me. I only need to open to what is there. My true nature, restored by Christ, is kind. When I open to the depths of my being, my true nature will emerge. I will live more fully in conformity to the image in which I was created. I will become more completely the person I most truly am.

You do not have to work to produce fruit. You need only to allow the natural fruit, contained in the seed from which the tree came, to be produced. The fruit of the Spirit are not another set of impossible standards to measure up to. The fruit of the Spirit are a description of who you truly are. The challenge Paul gives us in Galatians is to open to our true nature and live as the people we were created to be. You are kind. Be what you are.

The Complexities of Kindness

Being kind can be a complicated matter. There are at least two particular challenges in kindness. First, certain actions, which may initially appear kind, may turn out not to be kind at all. Second, some situations may suggest that there are limits to kindness.

I recently heard a sad story of kindness gone wrong. Tierra del Fuego is a series of islands off the southern tip of Argentina and Chile. These islands were explored in 1520 by the Spanish explorer Ferdinand Magellan. In the accounts of Magellan's trip to Tierra del Fuego, the writers say that he "discovered" these islands. The inhabitants who were already there, of course, may not have known that their home needed to be discovered. The islands were already populated by the Ona, Alakaluf, and Yahgan peoples. They had lived on these islands for generations, in harmony with their often difficult environment. Even in the harshest winter weather they wore hardly any clothing and travelled over the snowy land in bare feet.

In the late nineteenth century, explorers and missionaries from Europe, Argentina, and Chile were drawn to Tierra del Fuego in the hopes of finding gold and making converts. In kindness, these new arrivals provided clothing and more substantial housing for the inhabitants. The outcome was not what the new arrivals expected. Between 1850 and 1910 the original population of Tierra del Fuego was reduced by 85% to 90%. If you travel to these islands today, you will find no trace of the indigenous peoples. The original inhabitants, weakened by the innovations introduced by their visitors, and by unfamiliar foreign diseases, all died in the space of about sixty years. The kindness of housing and clothing proved to be a liability to the people of Tierra del Fuego. Sometimes what looks like kindness may not be all that kind.

The other caution about kindness is to remember that kindness is not weakness. It is easy to get the impression that, if I am kind, I will simply become a doormat for every abusive person who enters my life. If I choose kindness, will I never be able to stand up for myself or for another person? An entire culture was wiped out in Tierra del Fuego because no one had the power or the insight to say No to the influx of foreign ways. It is worth asking whether it might not have been more kind for someone, at some point, to resist the intervention of those who came to help the vulnerable peoples of these islands.

In Matthew chapter 11, Jesus gives us a picture of kindness that may help with these difficult challenges. This is one of the few places in the synoptic gospels where Jesus gives a picture of how he views himself. In describing himself, Jesus uses the word kind in a strange way. In chapter 11 verse 30, Jesus says, "My yoke is easy and my burden is light."

The word translated "easy" is the same Greek word Paul uses in Galatians 5:22 for the fifth fruit of the Spirit. So Jesus' statement at the end of Matthew 11:30 could be translated as "my yoke is kind." What sort of yoke is a "kind" yoke? To answer this question, we need to read Jesus' statement in a slightly larger context. In Matthew 11:28–30, Jesus says,

> Come to me, all you that are weary and are carrying heavy burdens, and I will give you rest. Take my yoke upon you, and learn from me; for I am gentle and humble in heart, and you will find rest for your souls. For my yoke is easy, and my burden is light (Matthew 11:28–30).

Jesus calls to himself those who are "weary and are carrying heavy burdens." The word translated "weary" means "working hard, toiling, striving, struggling." When we work hard, toil, strive, and struggle, there is a pretty good chance we will become weary.

When we are weary, we want rest. We hope that our burden will be relieved. We want a break. We hope that the pressures of life will let up. We long for a little bit of space, some breathing room just to relax and be at peace. This is exactly what Jesus promised to provide. "Come to me, all you that are weary and are carrying heavy burdens, and I will give you rest."

But if we are to receive the rest Jesus offers, we must do something. Jesus instructs those who would receive his rest to "Take my yoke upon you, and learn from me." To accept a yoke from another person is to be connected to that person and to conform the rhythm of our lives to the rhythm of the life of the one to whom we are yoked. The reason being yoked to Jesus brings rest is that Jesus is "gentle and humble in heart." Jesus' yoke is "kind." By being yoked to Jesus, "you will find rest for your souls." So a "kind" yoke is one that relieves the pressure of carrying the burdens of life.

To be kind is to be a source of rest for another person. To be kind is to share someone's burden. To be kind is to lighten the other person's load. This is often exactly the opposite of how we respond to people. Much of the time, rather than taking another person's burden away, we add burdens of our own.

The only other place in the gospels where the word "burden" appears is in Matthew 23:4. Jesus, speaking of the Scribes and Pharisees, says, "They tie up heavy burdens, hard to bear, and lay them on the shoulders of others; but they themselves are unwilling to lift a finger to move them." This is the opposite of kindness. The Scribes and Pharisees believed they knew how the rest of the world ought to operate. They thought they knew what was best for others, how other people should conduct their lives.

The Scribes and Pharisees were like the nineteenth-century explorers coming to Tierra del Fuego. Because they thought they knew what was best, they did not take the time to observe the original population. The foreigners were not able to learn from the wisdom of those who had lived in that harsh land for generations. The new arrivals forced practices upon the indigenous peoples that led ultimately to their destruction.

It intrigues and disturbs me that the people Jesus uses to illustrate the opposite of kindness are the religious people of his day. Churches can be the worst offenders when it comes to creating burdens. We join the Scribes and Pharisees whenever we are determined that we alone know what is best for another person.

Church should be the one place in the world where we do not feel that our burdens are increased. In church we should experience an air of lightness and ease, an atmosphere of openness and acceptance. This is the environment kindness creates. It is an atmosphere in which it is possible for people to rest, to be refreshed, to open, and to experience the freedom and peace given to us by Christ. It is an environment in which all people should feel heard and accepted.

Kindness creates a space in which I am able to listen more deeply to another. And when I listen more deeply, I am able to respond more appropriately to the other. Kindness takes the time to ask, "What is really going on here?" Kindness wants to know who this person really is. Why is this person responding in this way? What is happening in this person's life that has caused them to choose such behaviour?

Kindness does not try to change the other person, does not have an agenda for the other person's life. Kindness welcomes the other in all their troubling difference and strangeness, without demanding that the other conform to my vision for the other's behaviour. Kindness does not pretend that the other person's behaviour is not difficult and even painful. Kindness opens within me a place that is deeper and stronger than the pain of being in relationship with the other. It is from this deeper place that kindness discovers how to act appropriately in response to the person I experience as difficult.

When I accept another person in this way, I discover in the other's differences the gifts they have to offer to me. I realize the truth God desires to speak to me through the other, and I know how to respond with true kindness. When I shut the other down by burdening him or her with my demands, expectations, and presumed expertise, I cannot truly hear this person, or know who this person really is. And I cannot then respond with true kindness.

But we need to be careful here. Kindness is not just passive acceptance of every circumstance. When we define kindness as openness and acceptance of what is, we might get the impression that kindness means simply allowing ourselves to be run over by every powerful force that comes along. What might kindness have meant for the people of Tierra del Fuego toward the colonizing powers of Europe and South America?

Remember Jesus said, "Love your enemies, do good to those who hate you, bless those who curse you, pray for those who abuse you" (Luke 6:27–28). Does this mean that the people of Tierra del Fuego should have simply laid down under the onslaught of colonization? What might it mean for the victims in this story to love their enemies and "do good to those who hate you"? It is probably not kind to anyone to allow the violent abuser to continue in his destructive behaviour.

Kindness, as Jesus demonstrated, is not passive. In complaining about the Pharisees, Jesus said that they "are unwilling to lift a finger to move" the burdens people are carrying. Kindness means actively relieving another person of the burdens they bear. To be kind is to be willing "to lift a finger to move" the burden that is crushing another person.

We need to realize that the victim is not the only one carrying a burden. The violent abusive colonizers also carry a burden that is destroying them. To "pray for those who abuse you" is to pray that they might recognize their burden and allow those they are victimizing to participate in helping them be freed of their burdens.

The one in power will begin to be whole only when he comes to recognize the burden of his power and when he can ask forgiveness of those whom his power has hurt. What this might mean in any given situation is impossible to prescribe. Only the victim can learn in his or her own heart what it might mean to lift the burden from the shoulders of the abuser. It is only when we see that we have a role to play, even a power in the lives of those who have abused us, that we truly stop being victims.

So true kindness opens up space for everyone. True kindness empowers even those who may appear powerless. Kindness allows us all to connect with that which is true about ourselves and to share in freeing one another from the burdens we bear.

Everyone is capable of kindness. Everyone has a role to play in relieving the burdens of guilt and oppression that cause people to become weary. Kindness lives from a deep inner place of freedom and is guided by God's Spirit to take whatever action is truly kind in any situation.

Generosity —
Living From Fullness

If you take almost any portion of scripture and compare a number of translations, you will find many places where the English translations differ. One place this is less true than most is in Paul's list of the fruit of the Holy Spirit. In six major translations, six of the nine fruit are all translated using the same English words. Of the three fruit that have some variation, the differences are minor and usually occur in only one of the translations.

One of the places where there is a slight difference among translators occurs in fruit number six, where four out of six translators render the Greek word *agathosune* as "goodness." Only the *New Revised Standard Version* and the J. B. Phillips paraphrase have a different English word for fruit number six.

"Goodness" is an accurate translation of the Greek word *agathosune*. But it is an unfortunate choice. "Goodness" is a noun created by taking the adjective good and adding the suffix "ness." The suffix "ness" is added to words to indicate a state of being. So "goodness" is used to describe the state of being "good."

When we say that someone is a "good" person, we usually mean they do kind things for others — that is, they are in a state of being good, and their behaviour reflects this fact. To say that a person is "good" does not tell us much about the person or their behaviour. We say, "Oh, that is a 'good' idea." Or, "You did a 'good' job." It is not a great job, or magnificent, or fantastic. It is just good. We say "good day." And we do not really mean anything. We say, "For goodness' sake," which is a softened form of "For God's sake." God and goodness are also often replaced by the slang "gosh!" And if we are talking slang, we may be worried that "heck" is where we will go if we don't believe in "gosh." "Good" is a rather pale, ineffectual word.

The translators of the *New Revised Standard Version* of the Bible and the venerable J. B. Phillips must have felt that "good" did not really carry much weight as one of the fruit of the Spirit. So they both chose to translate the Greek word *agathosune* not as "goodness" but as "generosity." There is nothing pale about the word "generosity." "Generosity" is a big challenging word.

Jesus used the word "generous" in a story picture to talk about the nature of God. In Matthew chapter 20, Jesus told the story of a landowner who owned a vineyard and went into the marketplace early in the morning to hire labourers to work in his vineyard. The vineyard owner agreed with the workers on a salary, and they went to work for the day. Later the owner of the vineyard went and hired more workers. Four more times, as the day wore on, he went out and hired additional labourers. At the end of the day, the boss called those who were hired last and paid them first. When those hired first who had worked all day came to be paid, they were dismayed to be paid the same as those who had worked for only one hour. They grumbled against the vineyard owner, who replied to their complaint asking, "Are you envious because I am generous?" (Matthew 20:15).

Jesus used the picture of this vineyard owner to describe the nature of God. God is generous. When we are generous, we are like God. Generosity does not calculate the hours worked. It does not follow the dictates or standards of conventional behaviour. Generosity is not pinched or tight. It does not divide the world into winners and losers. Generosity takes a radically different and challenging view of life from that which characterizes most of the world.

The ancient desert literature of the early Christian church is full of pictures of generosity. One of my favourites from the desert tradition tells the story of two elders getting their baskets ready to sell in the city on market day.

Another old man had finished making his baskets for market when he heard a monk saying, "What shall I do, for the fair day is near, and I have no handles to finish my baskets?" The old man whose baskets were finished took the handles off his baskets and brought them to his brother saying, "Look, I have these handles to spare, take them and put them on your baskets." So for the great love that he had the old man caused his brother's work to succeed by neglecting his own.[12]

The beauty of this story is that the old man who had done his work did not administer a moralistic little lecture along with his gift. He did not feel that it was necessary to set his brother straight or to ask his brother why he had not been more careful with his time, or more disciplined in his work. The generous brother just gave freely without strings attached, without any accompanying demand or condition. The old man's explanation of why he was able to give away his basket handles is important. He says, "I have these handles to spare." He is saying, "I have an abundance." Generosity comes from having an experience of abundance. Generosity does not need to hold on, to cling, or to calculate, because generosity knows that there is always an overabundance of resources.

Sadly we often operate from a different place — from a position of scarcity. We believe that the available resources are limited; there is not enough to go around. The demands are too great, the needs too overwhelming. We do not have what it takes to meet the task at hand. So we feel we must harbour our resources. We must protect our interests, keep safe our assets, and never let anyone take advantage of us in case they take so much that

12 Helen Waddell (trans.), *The Desert Fathers* (New York: Vintage Books, 1998), p. 150.

there is nothing left for us. When we feel short-changed by life, we always hold back from giving.

When we are infected by the spirit of scarcity, we approach life with a cautious, tentative, uncertain, frightened attitude. When we operate from scarcity, we are often critical and negative, and look for what is wrong. Scarcity always starts with No. Scarcity always has a reason why this will not work, or that is not a good idea. Belief in scarcity destroys creativity and hinders the freedom of God's Spirit to work in our lives.

Ironically, no one ever really feels safe when we are operating in the cautious, protective mode of scarcity. Caution creates uncertainty. Everyone starts watching their behaviour, worried they might do the wrong thing or get the wrong answer.

I remember once hearing a person ask someone in a position of authority where they should place a gift for decorating the church. The person in authority replied, "I don't know. Why are you asking me? Put it wherever you like." Then after a short pause, the person added, "Anyway, if you put it in the wrong place, I will just move it." The first response appeared generous and expansive. It invited the person to place their gift wherever they felt was best. The second statement came from scarcity. It suggests that there is always a right and a wrong way to do things. And you had better do things the right way or there will be some terrible consequence. You have to figure out the rules in order to belong. Generosity simply receives the gift and embraces it with joy. There is no right or wrong place to put a gift.

Jesus was less concerned about doing things the right way. Jesus did not seem to feel the need for propriety. Jesus embraced whatever came with acceptance and welcome. Jesus did not need to hold back. He did not judge and evaluate.

Jesus was able to be generous because he knew that generosity never runs out. Generosity lives from an awareness of abundance, and knows that we have absolutely everything we need to fulfill any task that we have been called to by God. We do not need to save our resources or protect our assets. We have been filled with an absolute abundance by the living presence of God.

Jesus described generosity in Luke 6, when he said that, "A good measure, pressed down, shaken together, running over, will be put into your lap" (Luke 6:38). Generosity is "running over." It cannot be contained. It flows out from an endless wellspring of life, vitality, and energy. Because generosity is inexhaustible, it can afford to give and give and give.

Father Ivan Nicoletto in a sermon preached at the Christian ashram Shantivanam in India said, "Jesus, through actions and words, manifests to us a God who is excessive and boundless, unexpected and passionate."[13] This is the image of God we need to keep in our hearts, the reality of life we need to experience. We need to live from an awareness of "a God who is excessive" to the point of irresponsibility. God has poured the gifts of grace and presence into all lives regardless of merit, responsibility, or qualification.

In Luke chapter 15, Jesus presents another picture of the generosity of God, using a story of two brothers. The younger brother is an irresponsible, immature, reckless boy who comes to his father asking for his inheritance. Had I been the father in this story, knowing my son's character, I would have at least put the inheritance in trust until I was confident my son was mature enough to handle the responsibility. But I am not a good picture of God.

The father in the story of the Prodigal Son simply gives his son the money and allows the son to travel "to a distant country," where he squanders "his property in dissolute living" (Luke 15:13). And when the son is finally destitute and returns home, the father does not say, "I knew you could not handle

---

13 From Father Nicoletto's personal sermon notes.

this responsibility." The father simply opens his arms, embraces his son, and welcomes him with a joyful celebration. The father lavishes generosity upon this irresponsible son without punishment or recrimination.

This is the generosity of God. God's generosity is expansive and wide. It opens and welcomes. It draws in the one who knows that he does not measure up and does not deserve to be embraced. The older, responsible son in the story is offended by this kind of generosity. He cannot tolerate his father's response and shuts himself away from the celebration of God's graciousness and generosity: "He became angry and refused to go in" (Luke 15:28).

It is easy to be upset by God's generosity. It does not seem fair that those who have not worked as hard as we have, or been as responsible as we have been, should have blessings showered upon them. We want them to suffer. We want them to see how good we have been, how hard we have worked. And we want them to see that our good behaviour has resulted in us receiving special reward. We are unable to accept God's incredible generosity because we feel that something is lacking in our own lives and we want compensation.

But in Ephesians chapter 3, the writer prays for the recipients of his letter that they

> may have the power to comprehend, with all the saints,
> what is the breadth and length and height and depth,
> and to know the love of Christ that surpasses knowledge,
> so that you may be filled with all the fullness of God
> (Ephesians 3:18–19).

The testimony of the New Testament is that we have been "filled with all the fullness of God." We have received "the breadth and length and height and depth" of God's loving mercy in our lives. We need only to live from this awareness of fullness. How are we going to come to this experience of fullness?

This is not something we can aim at directly. We come to an awareness of fullness by a process of subtraction, not addition. We are able to discover that there is nothing more we need only when we let go of all those things we have ever held on to other than the one thing that we truly need and desire. We realize the fullness of God's presence when we stop cluttering the space of our spirits with things other than God. Our only task is to clear the space by letting go of the distractions, attachments, and obsessions that fill our inner space. When we empty ourselves of our need to create a sense of security and safety, we discover the One in whom we can find true safety and absolute security.

When a glass is full of pebbles, there is no room for the water. When the pebbles are emptied out, the water runs into the glass without impediment. The thirteenth-century poet Rumi uses the image of a lute to describe the truth of the fullness that is discovered in emptiness. In Coleman Barks's translation Rumi says,

> There's hidden sweetness in the stomach's emptiness.
> We are lutes, no more, no less. If the soundbox
> is stuffed full of anything, no music.[14]

Jesus asks his followers to empty out the obstacles in their lives that stand in the way of realizing the fullness of his presence. He instructs them to come to him empty-handed. He uses the curious image of a camel passing through the eye of a needle to make his point. When his disciples are shocked that Jesus has said, "it will be hard for a rich person to enter the kingdom of heaven," he explains using picture language, "Again I tell you, it is easier for a camel to go through the eye of a needle than for

---

14 Coleman Barks (trans.), *The Essential Rumi* (San Francisco: Harper, 1995), p. 69.

someone who is rich to enter the kingdom of God" (Matthew 19:23–24). To be "rich" in this context is to be cluttered, to be full with one's possessions. The camel needs to become so small that there is nothing left but the presence of God. Then the camel, divested of all other attachments, can pass easily "through the eye of a needle."

There are many ways to be rich. We can be rich in material benefits. Or we can be rich in talent, skill, physical health, or attractiveness. There is nothing inherently wrong with any of these things in themselves. But those who are rich in such things may find it more difficult to let them go. The more we have, the more there is for us to surrender in order to make ourselves small enough to pass "through the eye of a needle" into "the kingdom of heaven." Anything we cannot let go hinders our awareness of the fullness of God given to us by God's gracious, freely poured out Spirit.

Generosity becomes possible only when we lay aside everything other than the living presence of God. The generous person has nothing left to protect; everything has already been surrendered. The generous person lives from fullness. There is always enough to share, always enough to go around for everyone. All any of us wants is that inner assurance of God's fullness welling up within and pouring out to embrace all of life.

Building With Faithfulness

Paul uses the Greek word *pistis* for the seventh fruit of the Spirit. *Pistis* appears as a noun or an adjective more than 300 times in the New Testament. Most commonly it is translated as "faith." When we think of "faith," we tend to think in terms of something we believe. We speak of "the Christian faith," and we think of it as a certain set of intellectual propositions about the nature of life, God, and the human condition to which, as Christians, we choose to agree.

In the Anglican *Book of Alternative Services*, the celebrant at the eucharist calls the congregation to join in the recitation of one of the creeds of the church by saying, "Let us confess our faith." This risks giving the impression that faith is primarily about words, only something we "confess" with our lips.

This is not how Jesus understood *pistis*. Jesus never asked anyone to assent to any doctrines or to affirm a particular set of ideas. In fact, for Jesus it was the very people who most firmly held all the right doctrines and beliefs about God who seemed to be the furthest from true faith. And it was those people whose theology was lacking who seem to have been the closest to having a living relationship with God.

In Matthew chapter 8, Jesus meets a Roman centurion who has a sick servant. A centurion in the Roman army was responsible for keeping discipline among his soldiers. You did not become a Roman centurion in Jesus' day without being accustomed to violence and brutality. The life of the average Roman centurion probably did not include much concern for the finer points of ethics or spirituality.

And yet, speaking of the centurion he meets in Matthew chapter 8, Jesus says, "Truly I tell you, in no one in Israel have I found such faith" (Matthew 8:10). Clearly, for Jesus, faith is something much more than having right doctrine. The centurion did believe something that was true about Jesus. He believed Jesus could heal his servant. So the faith Jesus found in the centurion was something the centurion believed, but it was also something he lived. Faithfulness is a way of living in tune with what is true.

There is an interesting picture of faith later on in Matthew's gospel, in chapter 25. Jesus is telling the parable of the talents. Three slaves are entrusted with different sums of money while their master goes on a trip. When the master returns, two of the slaves give the master back his original investment plus the profits they have made. The third slave has made no profit from the master's investment and simply returns to his master the coin he was originally given.

When the master receives his investment and the profit from the first slave, he says, "Well done, good and trustworthy slave; you have been trustworthy in a few things, I will put you in charge of many things" (Matthew 25:21). The word translated here as "trustworthy" is the same word Paul uses for the seventh fruit of the Spirit. These slaves believed that their master had entrusted them with a sacred trust. And they acted upon this belief. Their faithfulness was demonstrated in the way they lived in relationship with their master.

The third slave did nothing with his master's investment. This slave says, "Master, I knew that you were a harsh man, reaping where you did not sow, and gathering where you did not scatter seed; so I was afraid, and I went and hid your talent in the ground" (Matthew 25:24–25). He believed something that was untrue about his master, and so he became fearful. His fear paralysed him, and he was unable to live a life of faithfulness.

So faithfulness asks us to believe what is true and then to live in tune with that belief.

There is a wonderful poem by Wendell Barry that describes beautifully what faithfulness looks like. Barry uses the image of a wild rose bush to speak about his relationship to his wife. The bush has always been present at the edge of the woods where Barry is in the habit of taking his daily walk. One day, as he is walking by, Barry notices that the bush has burst into flower. The poem says,

> Sometimes hidden from me
> in daily custom and in trust,
> so that I live by you unaware
> as by the beating of my heart,
>
> suddenly you flare in my sight,
> a wild rose blooming at the edge
> of thicket, grace and light
> where yesterday was only shade,
>
> and once more I am blessed, choosing
> again what I chose before.

This is faithfulness — "choosing / again what I chose before." Faithfulness is choosing over and over to go in the same direction, the direction you chose when you were able to see what was true and good and right. Faithfulness is choosing that thing that you know corresponds with the highest and best purposes God has for your life. And it is this choosing that enables us to see "grace and light" where we might never have noticed it before.

The problem with our culture is that we are always running after something else, something more, something better, bigger, faster, flashier. And so we miss the beauty that is right here. We miss the beauty of the ordinary, of the daily routine, the beauty of those people who are so familiar that we have stopped even noticing them. Faithfulness opens our eyes so that we can begin to truly see.

Early one Sunday morning many years ago in Manitoba, I was sitting in the living room of the rectory next door to the church where I was the rector. It was probably forty below outside. The wind was blowing, the snow was deep on the ground, and more snow was falling. I sat looking out the window thinking, "Well, there probably will not be anyone in church this morning, and there certainly will not be an 8:00 A.M. congregation."

At that moment, walking down the middle of the road in knee-deep fresh snow, a woman was approaching the church. As soon as I saw her, I knew she was the volunteer appointed to prepare the altar for the 8:00 A.M. communion service and that, after she had set up, she would sit down in a pew and wait patiently for me to arrive to lead the service. This is faithfulness.

To be faithful is to be solid and steady, rooted and grounded. A faithful person is one who is reliable and constant, a person you can count on. Faithfulness just keeps showing up. It does not come and go depending on how the situation feels. Faithfulness has learned to live beyond likes and dislikes. It does not go up when things are going well and down when things are going badly. It stays steady, regardless of what the weather may be doing. Faithfulness does not depend on the whim of the moment. It does not give up when the going gets difficult or quit just because things become uncomfortable or awkward. Faithfulness chooses to keep on and on, and on and on. It is predictable, reliable, and trustworthy no matter what may be going on in the external world of one's circumstances.

As with all the fruit of the Spirit, it is important to keep in mind that faithfulness is not something we are able to produce by ourselves. It is a fruit of God's Spirit, produced in us by the mysterious secret working of God's Spirit in our being. But there may be something we can do to prepare ourselves to be able to produce this fruit of God's Spirit.

In Luke chapter six, Jesus speaks to his disciples, describing people who hear his word and do what he tells them.

I will show you what someone is like who comes to me, hears my words, and acts on them. That one is like a man building a house, who dug deeply and laid the foundation on rock; when a flood arose, the river burst against that house but could not shake it, because it had been well built. But the one who hears and does not act is like a man who built a house on the ground without a foundation. When the river burst against it, immediately it fell, and great was the ruin of that house (Luke 6:47-49).

Fix this image in your mind — "a man building a house" that is going to be able to stand when a flood rises and the river bursts against it. This is the kind of house we all want, one that will stand steady and strong in the midst of the storms, uncertainties, and confusions that life inevitably brings. We do not want a house that will collapse at the first sign of difficulty or struggle, that "when the river burst against it, immediately it fell, and great was the ruin of that house."

If we are going to build a house that will stand in the storms, we must dig deeply and lay the foundation for our house on rock. We can prepare ourselves to receive the gift of faithfulness by digging down deeply into our lives and laying a solid foundation. We need to scrape away the unstable topsoil, to pull out the roots and small stones that prevent us from getting down to bedrock. This is the way we find the solid rock on which the steady building of faithfulness can be constructed.

We need to know that this bedrock does exist. There is a steady, stable, strong place within our being. The challenge of the spiritual life is to find this place of bedrock and live from there, rather than from the constantly changing, uneasy tumult of feelings and circumstances. There are so many things in life that can throw us off balance, so many forces at work in the world around us that can cause us to believe things that are false or to fail to live in tune with what we know to be true.

The slave in the parable of the talents who buried his master's money was not a bad person. He was a person who listened to his fears and allowed his fears to be the dominant reality of his life. He looked out at the world around him and concluded that the world is an unsafe, insecure, uncertain place. He was right about that.

But this is where he made his mistake. In response to the uncertainty and insecurity of life, he concluded that the only logical response was to hide. He buried the gift he had been given in a futile attempt to keep himself safe from all those forces of uncertainty and chaos he experienced. The other two slaves knew there was a dimension to life that was deeper and more true than all the uncertainty, doubt, and insecurity they might ever experience. And so they were able to live a life of faithfulness.

The call of faithfulness is the call to find that place within ourselves that is deeper than our fears, the place that is deeper than feeling, deeper than uncertainty and insecurity, deeper than the chaos and confusion that characterize so much of the surface of our lives. There is a deeper place. There is a more solid ground upon which to live. When we live from this steady place, we make good decisions for our lives and for the lives of those around us.

There may be times when faithfulness calls us to walk away from a certain situation. But we can only know when faithfulness means walking away if we have first spent time in that deep, quiet grounded place of God's presence.

We need to find the awareness that knows that it knows that it knows. This consciousness is beyond rational thinking or our grasp of the intricacies of Christian theology. It is deeper than our feelings and deeper than all the inherited messages we carry along with us from our past. It transcends social conditioning or external expectation. It is the place in which we discover that freedom Paul speaks about when he says, "For freedom Christ has set us free. Stand firm, therefore, and do not submit again to a yoke of slavery" (Galatians 5:1). To be free, we must first stand firm. We must find that place of stability and strength that is the true centre of our being.

Near the end of his First Letter to the Corinthians, Paul urges his audience to continue in their ministry together. He says, "Therefore, my beloved, be steadfast, immovable, always excelling in the work of the Lord, because you know that in the Lord your labour is not in vain" (1 Corinthians 15:58). A life that is lived "in the Lord" is a life that has found the place that is "steadfast" and "immovable." It is a life that cannot be shaken. Faithfulness starts in this place that is not shakeable, that cannot be moved by fickle circumstance. This is the place where God guides us into a life of faithfulness.

Rest in this place within yourself. Then you will be able to participate in holding the universe together and providing space for life to be born.

A Gentleness Manifesto (Part 1)

Gentleness is a relationship word. It has to do with how we relate to another, in whatever form we encounter the other. Gentleness can apply to our relationships with people or, equally, to our relationships with other parts of Creation.

Many of the interactions that take place in the world around us are characterized not by gentleness but by violence. The violence of our relationship with another may be extremely subtle. Violence does not always take the form of guns and bombs. Violence can occur in the words or tone of voice we use, the attitudes with which we approach another, or our silent actions and behaviours. Whenever we devalue the other, treat the other as an object, or use the other to meet our own needs, we are guilty of violence.

Our culture does not always value gentleness. We tend to reward people who have the ability to impose their will on others and who can get the job done no matter what obstacles they may have to crush in the process. Gentleness will probably never achieve great "success" in the world. If we understand gentleness properly, however, we will discover that it is a strong, life-giving quality.

Gentleness is a quality that, perhaps more than any other, describes the way Jesus interacted with the world. He said of himself, "I am gentle (*praos*) and humble in heart" (Matthew 11:29). And when Jesus entered Jerusalem in a triumphal victory procession, he was described as a king "who comes to you, gentle (*praos*) and riding on a donkey" (Matthew 21:5 NIV).

What follows is a ten-point "Gentleness Manifesto," a declaration of the qualities I believe are characteristic of gentleness. I will seek to outline what true gentleness might look like and how this quality was demonstrated by, or taught in, Jesus' life and ministry.

Before looking at the nature of gentleness, it is important to understand that, in his life and teaching, Jesus was not formulating social or organizational policy. Societies and organizations have a responsibility to implement laws by which human conduct is governed. These laws aim to preserve the greatest well-being for the greatest number of people. There may be times when force is necessary to preserve the stability of a social group. Jesus did not say how the principles of gentleness should be enacted in a society. It is left to our wisdom and vision to discover together how the qualities of gentleness should inform the principles by which we govern our social interactions.

We will look at the characteristics of gentleness in two parts — first, at five attitudes or behaviours which gentleness will avoid; second, at five positive attitudes or behaviours toward which gentleness will tend.

1. I will not push another where the other is not able or willing to go.

In Mark 10, a rich young man approached Jesus asking, "Good teacher, what must I do to inherit eternal life?'" (Mark 10:17). It appears that this young man was a fine moral person. When Jesus instructed him to abide by the requirements of the law, the young man replied, "Teacher, I have kept all these since my youth" (Mark 10:20).

It is an outrageous claim to state that one has faithfully "kept" all the requirements of God's law since one's youth. But Jesus does not ridicule or mock the young man. He does not give a little lecture pointing out errors in the young man's understanding or places in his life where he has fallen short of God's law. He simply says to the rich young man, "You lack one thing; go, sell what you own, and give the money to the poor" (Mark 10:21). Then Mark says, when the young man "heard this, he was shocked and went away grieving, for he had many possessions" (Mark 10:22).

At this point in the story, many of us might have chased after the young man, trying to convince him to change his ways, encouraging him to reconsider. Jesus does not chase after the young man. He does not call out to him, blame him, berate him, badger him, or try to convince him. Jesus simply lets the young man go.

It is not that Jesus did not care about this young man. Mark says that, when the young man spoke, "Jesus, looking at him, loved him" (Mark 10:21). Jesus was simply not willing to demand that this young man do something he did not feel able to do. He would not attempt to push this young man where he was not willing to go. Jesus knew that any decision arrived at under coercion is not a decision that is freely made and, therefore, cannot be an expression of love. Choices made from pressure come from violence and lead to more violence. Only choices that are freely made come from gentleness and lead to gentleness.

In the church it is common to hear talk about commitment, responsibility, and faithfulness. These are important qualities. But such words often cover manipulation, abuse, and violence. These words can be the means we use to attempt to push people into jobs, giving, or involvement that they do not feel compelled within themselves to offer. Gentleness emerges in a community only where individuals are permitted to respond freely to the inward stirring of God's Spirit.

Jesus believed that "the Father who dwells in me does his works" (John 14:10). God is the worker. As Paul knew, "I planted, Apollos watered, but God gave the growth" (1 Corinthians 3:6). Gentleness comes when we trust that God is growing the fruit of the Spirit in the lives of each person. Gentleness grows when we give up trying to be the Holy Spirit in one another's lives.

2. I will not use the other to fulfill my own needs, demands, or desires.

Before his public ministry began, Jesus was "led up by the Spirit into the wilderness to be tempted by the devil" (Matthew 4:1). After forty days and forty nights Jesus "was famished." He had a deep longing, a legitimate need, and a powerful desire to receive physical nourishment. Jesus also had the power to satisfy his desire for food. And so "the tempter came and said to him, 'If you are the Son of God, command these stones to become loaves of bread'" (Matthew 4:3). The temptation is for Jesus to exercise his own power on the stones and change them into bread in order to meet his needs and desires. Jesus is being tempted to use something outside himself to satisfy his own longing.

Jesus replies to the tempter, saying, "One does not live by bread alone, but by every word that comes from the mouth of God" (Matthew 4:4). Jesus understood that we can never fulfill our deepest longings by anything external to ourselves. He demonstrated that the path to gentleness lies along the way of recognizing that our desires can be fulfilled only by living in relationship with God.

As the anonymous author of the fourteenth-century English spiritual classic *The Cloud of Unknowing* says, "To those who have been made perfectly humble, nothing shall be lacking, not a physical thing and not a spiritual thing. And why? Because they have God in whom all plenty is; and whoever has Him — yes, as this book says — needs nothing else in this life."[15] The way to

---

15 Ira Progroff (trans.), *The Cloud of Unknowing* (New York: Dell Publishing, 1957), p.118.

gentleness is found by those who learn that they have all they need in God.

When we impose our needs, demands, and desires on others, in an attempt to fulfill an inner longing, we always do violence to them. We discover gentleness when we realize that others do not exist to satisfy our longings. We are opened to receive the fruit of gentleness when we set others free to be as they are and resist any temptation to try to meet our needs by using others.

3. I will not have expectations that another should be other than the other is.

Near the end of his life Jesus said to his closest friends and followers, "You will all become deserters; for it is written, 'I will strike the shepherd, and the sheep will be scattered' " (Mark 14:27). Jesus also foretold Peter's denial and the betrayal by Judas. Jesus did not expect that his friends would be different from what he knew they were. Most of us would have spent our time with these unreliable friends trying to change them, trying to encourage them to be different. Jesus simply accepted them as they were.

At the last supper Jesus came to each of his friends and demonstrated the depth of his welcome by washing the feet of each of his disciples. Jesus performed the lowliest act of a slave on the very night that his friends would desert, deny, and betray him.

Jesus did not have great expectations for his friends. He knew what was in them and was not surprised when they lived out of their weaker nature. Yet, despite their failures, despite the hurt they caused him, Jesus said to them, "I do not call you servants any longer, because the servant does not know what the master is doing; but I have called you friends" (John 15:15).

Jesus knew what was in the heart of each of these men when he first called them to become his followers. He understood how they would let him down, how terribly they would fail, how deeply they would wound him; but Jesus chose them anyway. Jesus knew they would be exactly who they turned out to be. He had no expectation they would be any different. And yet Jesus gave himself to them.

Expectations destroy gentleness. The world does not exist to meet my expectations. I have no right to expect anything from anyone, or from life. I may hope for responsibility, respect, and honesty. I may hope to be well treated and for my life to run along smoothly. But I have no right to expect that you will be anything other than what you are. I do not know what forces in your life have caused you to become the person you have become. I have never lived inside the particular biological, environmental, emotional, social mix that has created you. As much as I might desire to understand you and empathize with you, there is ultimately a great gulf fixed between us.

The great fourth-century mystic Gregory of Nyssa said that, "It is characteristic of divinity to be incomprehensible: this must also be true of the image."[16] Human beings are hemmed around on every side by mystery. Gentleness gives us the humility to accept one another as we are. There are deep forces that have brought each of us to the places in life to which we have come. There is a core of mystery at the heart of every human being that is not accessible to anyone but God, and perhaps to the person themselves. Our awareness of this mystery exists to give us the gift of humility in dealing with one another. Ultimately I do not know who you are or why you make the choices you make.

Gentleness requires that I lay down my expectations. Instead of making demands on another, the gentle person takes responsibility for his or her own responses to the other. Gentleness will

---

16 Quoted in Olivier Clement, *The Roots of Christian Mysticism* (New York: New York City Press, 1993), p. 78.

grow only as I stop expecting my circumstances to be different from what they are.

4. I will not resist or harden against the other even when I feel hurt.

If anyone ever had just cause to choose hardness and resistance, it was Jesus. But Jesus refused to respond to the harshness of the world by hardening his heart. Despite all the pain that awaited him in Jerusalem, Luke says, "When the days drew near for Jesus to be taken up, he set his face to go to Jerusalem" (Luke 9:51). Jesus opened to meet life as it was about to come to him. He did not resist his destiny. He did not fight against the inevitability of pain. Jesus refused to close himself or harden against life, even when life led him along the way of pain and sorrow.

Toward the end of his life Jesus entered Jerusalem for the last time, knowing he was going to suffer unspeakably, that he would be deserted by those closest to him and would be mocked, ridiculed, and finally brutally executed by those who despised him. Yet looking around at this city whose people were going to so brutally abuse him, Jesus did not call down God's wrath. He did not order his followers to rise up in righteous anger against the leaders and the violent injustice they were about to perpetrate. Instead Jesus lamented, saying, "Jerusalem, Jerusalem, the city that kills the prophets and stones those who are sent to it! How often have I desired to gather your children together as a hen gathers her brood under her wings" (Matthew 23:37).

Jesus is not a starry-eyed naïve innocent, believing that everyone will always turn out to be kind and loving. Jesus knew what was in the human heart. He knew the violence and hatred that were about to be poured on him. And yet Jesus responded with tenderness and compassion. He opened his heart again and again to those who were about to seek his destruction. Jesus did not close down. He did not try to protect himself. He responded from that place within himself that could be characterized only by the gentleness of a mother hen caring tenderly for her baby chicks.

When they mocked him, spat on him, beat him, and nailed him to the cross, Jesus said, "Father, forgive them; for they do not know what they are doing" (Luke 23:34). He refused to be drawn into their orbit of violence. Jesus turned away from the harshness of retribution, recrimination, and judgement. Instead Jesus continued to hold his heart open to those who abused him. He poured out forgiveness and love from the cross of torture. He did not give in to his own personal pain and allow it to shape his spirit. Jesus chose to transcend the horror of his circumstances and continue to open his heart to the suffering that life brought.

We always have a choice. We can resist and harden against another when the other is not fulfilling our expectations. If we choose to harden to another, we will increase the violence in the world. Or we can choose the way of gentleness. We can choose to open and soften to the circumstances of life as they are. This does not mean we will simply become a passive doormat to every unpleasantness life might bring. It means that we will be able to respond in a much more healthy, life-giving, and gentle manner to the reality of our circumstances as they present themselves. From a position of softness and openness it becomes possible to add more gentleness to the world.

If I pay attention to myself, I will become aware of those times when I am resisting and hardening against someone or something. I can feel it in my body. I can feel the tension, the pressure in my back that is a sure signal that I am putting up barriers to whatever I am facing.

Softness feels different from resistance. Softness is a warm opening toward what is. Softness embraces life as it comes and then responds to circumstances from a place of openness and embrace, rather than from a place of resistance and brace. When I respond from a braced hard position, I create violence. When I respond from softness and openness, I will not do nothing, but whatever I do will bring greater gentleness and freedom into the world with which I interact.

5. I will not blame another for my own unhappiness or discomfort.

When Jesus came to visit at the home of the sisters Martha and Mary, there was a great deal of work to be done. Martha "was distracted by her many tasks," and came to Jesus complaining of her sister, saying, "Lord, do you not care that my sister has left me to do all the work by myself?" (Luke 10:40). Martha blamed her discontent upon her sister. She believed her unhappiness could be solved if her sister would do a little more work around the house.

Jesus refused to accept Martha's determination to blame someone else for her unhappy state. Instead Jesus instructed Martha to look at her own inner condition. Jesus said, "Martha, Martha, you are worried and distracted by many things" (Luke 10:41). The problem is not somewhere out there. The problem is in your own heart.

Mary, Jesus says, "has chosen the better part, which will not be taken away from her" (Luke 10:42). The "better part" is sitting at Jesus' feet and listening to his teaching. Gentleness will be found by those who start by sitting in the presence of gentleness. Jesus is the gentle one, and those who stay with him will become like him. When we start from our worry and distraction, we will always end up by looking for someone or something out there to blame. When we start with the gentle spirit of Jesus, we will find that our hearts grow in gentleness and we bring more gentleness wherever we go.

It is easy to point the finger at another. But every discontent is a call to examine our own hearts, asking ourselves what we are unhappy about. Gentleness does not blame the other. Gentleness sees every discomfort as an opportunity for self-examination. Honest self-examination will always lead to greater gentleness and deeper openness to another, in all of the other's difference and challenge.

Mary sat at the feet of Jesus resting in the grace of his presence. As we choose to sit where Mary sat, we will find ourselves moved to perform acts of gentleness and will find the fruit of gentleness growing in our own lives.

A Gentleness Manifesto (Part 2)

6. I will trust and respect the integrity and goodwill of the other.

In Mark chapter three, Jesus calls twelve men and designates them "apostles." In the process of identifying these twelve people to fill this special role, Jesus gives three of them new names. The first apostle to be appointed is Simon, to whom Jesus gives the name "Peter." The Greek word for Peter is "petros," which means "rock." It is hard to imagine anyone less like a rock than Simon as he appears in the gospels. Impetuous and unpredictable, he crumbles in the face of danger and resorts to lies in order to protect himself. Simon seems more like a piece of bark riding the waves of the ocean than a steady rock in the midst of a stormy sea.

But Jesus looked more deeply into Simon's spirit and saw there the rock that Simon would become. Jesus was willing to look past the surface of Simon's unsteady behaviour and see the goodness and integrity that lay just below. Jesus trusted that, with the work of God's Holy Spirit, Simon's true character would be revealed and he would become the rock Jesus had named him at the beginning of their relationship. Jesus did not badger or browbeat Simon, pressuring him to change. He simply had confidence that God's Spirit would work in Simon and transform him into the person Jesus knew he could become.

Gentleness chooses to assume the best of another. Gentleness believes that the other is trying to find the way toward life, to live according to the best principles and understanding available. We may not understand another's behaviour, but we trust that, in whatever possibly confused and bewildered way, the other is struggling toward the light.

To be gentle is to refuse to judge. Gentleness always remembers that Jesus said, "Do not judge, and you will not be judged" (Luke 6:37). In John's gospel Jesus put this principle in even more challenging terms, saying, "I do not judge anyone who hears my words and does not keep them, for I came not to judge the world, but to save the world" (John 12:47). Jesus does not say here that he will not judge people who have never heard his word. Most of us would have no trouble with that idea. Jesus says here that he is not even going to judge those who hear his words but do not "keep them." Jesus will not even judge people who have heard the word of truth and choose to go a different way. This is a quality of gentleness that would challenge most of us.

To be gentle is to see in the other the true and deepest longing of the other's heart. Gentleness looks past surface behaviour, understanding that human beings are more than the things they do. Gentleness understands that even apparently unacceptable behaviour is only a cry for love, attention, and security. Violent, abusive behaviour comes from a place of pain and brokenness. So gentleness responds to the deeper movement in the heart of every person.

Because gentleness is willing to look beneath the surface, it is able to call forth whatever is more real and true from a person's being. Gentleness does not dwell on the shadow side, but views all behaviour as a manifestation of the human desire to move toward the light. As a friend of mine is fond of saying, "we are damaged goods, not damaged bads."

How we view another has a profound effect on the way we are able to be in relation to the other. When we look at another with trust and respect, it is more likely that we will draw from that person the kind of behaviour that is worthy of respect and merits trust. Jesus searched for the best in each person he met and helped them move toward greater wholeness. When we see the best in the other, there will be more gentleness in the world around us.

7. I will listen deeply to the other.

In Luke chapter eight, Jesus teaches the parable of the sower and the seed, which he concludes with the encouragement, "Let anyone with ears to hear listen!" (Luke 8:8). The passage is followed by an explanation in which Jesus describes the different ways that God's kingdom is received. After the explanation Jesus changes the metaphor, and uses the image of a lamp to show that the kingdom of God is intended to be seen. Then, after this slight detour into a discussion of seeing, Jesus returns to the idea of hearing and says, "Then pay attention to how you listen" (Luke 8:18). Careful listening is a deep discipline of the Christian faith.

Jesus listened carefully to those who came to him. He responded to deep needs, refusing to be drawn away by superficial concerns. Jesus listened to the heart, paying careful attention to what was really going on beneath the surface in his conversations and interactions. Because Jesus was willing to listen deeply, he was always able to respond appropriately with a word that opened something inside the person with whom he was engaged in conversation.

In John chapter four, when the woman of Samaria reported on her conversation with Jesus, she said, "Come and see a man who told me everything I have ever done!" (John 4:29). She felt known by Jesus. She knew she had been heard. He had paid attention to her, and in doing so Jesus had opened her to a new level of truth and life.

The writer of the Letter of James counsels his readers, saying, "You must understand this, my beloved: let everyone be quick to listen, slow to speak" (James 1:19). I have seldom regretted holding my tongue. I have often regretted speaking too quickly and too much. Gentleness listens before it speaks.

Listening is not easy work. It means more than just allowing another person to talk. It means creating an environment where the other has a chance to feel safe enough to truly speak. Listening means really paying attention, being careful to ensure that the other feels fully free to express what needs to be expressed.

Listening means I do not sit thinking up my next response while you speak. It means I want to understand you even more than I want to make my point or convince you that I am right. I want to know who you are. I want to be able to see the world from your point of view, to understand the world you live in, and appreciate what it is that makes your life work.

When we shut another down, or resist what another feels the need to say, we always create violence. Listening is a quiet, gentle discipline. When people know they have been listened to, gentleness will grow.

8. I will risk allowing my own sense of vulnerability to be seen by another.

In John chapter 11, Jesus receives a report that his friend Lazarus has died. When Jesus arrives at his friend's home, he asks, "Where have you laid him?" In response they say, "come and see." Then, John reports, "Jesus began to weep. So the Jews said, 'See how he loved him!'" (John 11:34–35). Jesus has been called to this scene as a great prophet, a respected man of learning. He is the one who should bring answers and solutions. Lazarus's family must have anticipated that Jesus would at least come and comfort them. And yet, on the way to his friend's tomb, Jesus simply weeps.

Jesus makes no attempt to hide his sorrow. He does not pretend to hold it all together. Jesus does not put on a fake smile; he does not present a façade of being in control of his emotions.

He does not stand impassively aside from the mourning of his friends for their beloved. Jesus enters fully into their sorrow and allows his own sense of heartbreak to be demonstrated for all to see. Jesus opens his heart and allows the tenderness to flow out. Even complete strangers witness Jesus' sorrow and in the process see the depth of love of which Jesus was capable.

Most of us spend our lives hiding who we truly are. We resist allowing our real feelings to be seen. We have been brought up to believe that we must repress our innermost emotions. Jesus was willing to allow his true self to be seen by anyone who was willing to look. Jesus lived as a person of true integrity and authenticity. Gentleness does not "fake it" or hide the sense of vulnerability we all experience at times. Gentleness is genuine. It is honest about deep feelings and willing to allow others to be honest about their experiences of life.

Gentleness is able to risk allowing its vulnerability to be seen by another, because those who practise gentleness experience the true strength of God. Those who practise gentleness know that there really is no vulnerability at the heart of our being. At the centre of who we are is the invincible living power of God that no one and nothing can take from us.

True gentleness is invincibly strong because it knows that there is nothing it needs to protect. Gentleness lives from that place of true power and is therefore willing to be seen no matter what feelings may be bubbling on the surface.

9. I will surrender my determination to control the other.

Near the end of his life, Jesus faced the ultimate challenge of surrender. He struggled in the Garden of Gethsemane with the horror of the fate he knew was coming. Jesus testified that he was "deeply grieved, even to death" (Matthew 26:38) by the approaching ordeal. Three times Jesus prayed that his lot might be changed. And yet each time he prayed also, "yet not what I want but what you want" (Matthew 26:39). This is an amazing picture of surrender to a will greater than his own, even when that will might run entirely contrary to the will of the one who is praying.

The picture of his surrender is made even more startling when we are reminded, by Jesus himself, that he had the power to change the outcome of this story if he chose. At the moment of his arrest, when Peter brandished his sword in an attempt to protect him, Jesus asks, "Do you think that I cannot appeal to my Father, and he will at once send me more than twelve legions of angels?" (Matthew 26:53). A legion in the Roman army of Jesus' day consisted of between three to six thousand men. Twelve legions of angels is unlimited power.

Jesus had all the power of God at his disposal, and he chose not to use it. He surrendered control from a position of power, not from a position of resignation and weakness. Gentleness is not defeat. Gentleness comes from a true inner strength. The gentle person is the one who knows his or her power and chooses to surrender control to God.

Surrender is the key to gentleness. Anything to which I cling creates hardness in my life. Anything I refuse to let go of will lead ultimately to violence. The way of gentleness lies along the path of letting go. I can let go of absolutely everything, because I know that when I have let go of all things, I continue to have the One who will never let go of me. Through the prophet Isaiah, God asks, "Can a woman forget her nursing child, or show no compassion for the child of her womb?" The answer follows immediately, "Even these may forget, yet I will not forget you" (Isaiah 49:15).

It makes sense to let go of everything because we are held by God. Deep within, we possess what really counts — the unquenchable Spirit of God. God does not fail. God does not let us down. The force of love and the power of the universe is the strength of faithfulness. We have nothing to fear. When we know this security and strength deep in our being, gentleness will rise from the depth and shape our entire lives.

The ultimate path to gentleness lies along the way of knowing that true security exists only in the permanence and hope that fill our lives by God's grace and mercy. The security that leads to gentleness lies in never forgetting the promise Jesus made to his friends when he said, "Remember, I am with you always, to the end of the age" (Matthew 28:20). The strength of the One who is with us is vastly greater than any forces that might come against us. We have within our being the unlimited power of God. There is nothing and no one that can crush that which lives within us.

Therefore, we can always choose gentleness. We can always soften, open, and receive. We do not need to fight our own battles. We do not need to stand up for ourselves. We can follow Jesus all the way to the cross and die to the power of the world. Then the gentleness of Jesus will be released in our spirits, and the world will be a less violent place.

10. I will follow the wind of God's Spirit wherever it may lead.

Any discussion of gentleness in relation to Jesus must acknowledge that not all of Jesus' words or actions may have felt gentle to those who witnessed them. Those who were on the receiving end of the "whip of cords," with which Jesus "drove all of them out of the temple, both the sheep and the cattle," and whose money he poured out and tables he overturned, may not have experienced Jesus as being particularly gentle (John 2:15). Those who found themselves directly addressed as "You snakes, you brood of vipers!" (Matthew 23:33) may be forgiven for thinking Jesus' words were less than gentle.

Gentleness is not weakness. When necessary, gentleness can be strong and decisive. Gentleness can act powerfully when circumstances require forceful action. The important question is where the actions or the words are coming from. Jesus said of himself, "Very truly, I tell you, the Son can do nothing on his own, but only what he sees the Father doing; for whatever the Father does, the Son does likewise" (John 5:19).

God never changes. So when we act or speak from that place within ourselves that is most deeply conscious of God, we will speak and act in ways that are consistent with God's presence. God's Spirit is gentle. We need to be careful when we attribute to Jesus the kind of emotions we expect would characterize our lives in a particular situation. Jesus in the temple casting out the moneychangers and the sellers is often portrayed as being angry.

There is only one place in all of the gospels where anger is directly associated with Jesus. In Mark chapter three, Jesus asks those in the synagogue if it is lawful to heal on the sabbath. When they refuse to answer, Mark says Jesus "looked around at them with anger." His anger, Mark says, came from the fact that Jesus was "grieved at their hardness of heart" (Mark 3:4–5). This is the same situation Jesus faced in the temple. Religious people, in the name of their religion, were placing obstacles in the way of other people finding the healing and wholeness God desired for them.

The temple scene is an acted out parable, demonstrating that anything that gets in the way of another person coming into the full awareness of God's loving presence must be swept aside. Jesus came to open the way to God. Everything that prevents this process must be removed. At times the removal of obstacles in our lives may feel violent and upsetting. But the motivation behind Jesus' actions and words was always his desire that a way might be clear for all human beings to enter fully into an awareness of God's life-giving presence. In the deepest place, even when he spoke harsh words and performed what might have appeared to be violent actions, Jesus moved from a place of gentleness.

In the First Letter of Peter, Peter instructs his readers to "let your adornment be the inner self with the lasting beauty of a gentle and quiet spirit, which is very precious in God's sight" (1 Peter 3:4). Gentleness is a quality born by God's Spirit in the "inner self" of our being. When we connect deeply with the reality of God's presence, we will discover the gentleness that is God. To be gentle is to live from that "inner self" of light and "lasting beauty."

Opening
to Gentleness

It is lovely to have a beautiful vision of what gentleness might look like in our lives. But gentleness is often not our instinctive response in many situations. We are inclined to close down in response to circumstances that are not to our liking. We tend naturally to put up barriers between ourselves and those things we perceive to be threatening or that make us feel uncomfortable. So the question is, How do we get from where we are to a place where we might more fully embody this quality of gentleness?

In response to this question we need to remember something we observed at the beginning of our discussion of gentleness. Describing himself in Matthew 11:29, Jesus said, "I am gentle and humble in heart." Then in John's gospel, when Jesus promised his disciples the gift of the Holy Spirit, he said, "You know him, because he abides with you, and he will be in you" (John 14:17b).

The Holy Spirit is the Spirit of Jesus who promised that his Spirit would live within his followers. So the Spirit of Jesus, who described himself as "gentle," lives in his followers. We do not have to get something that we do not already have. We have the gentleness of Jesus. We are only being challenged to give that which we already have.

The key to giving gentleness is to recognize that we cannot give to the other that which we have not already given to ourselves.

Gentleness toward others is only possible if we begin by being gentle toward ourselves. Paul says in Galatians 6:7, "Do not be deceived; God is not mocked, for you reap whatever you sow." This is true first of all in relation to our own lives. If I am bitter, resentful, and judgemental about my life, I will be bitter, resentful and judgemental about your life. Jesus said, "Out of the abundance of the heart the mouth speaks" (Matthew 12:34).

Whatever is in my heart toward myself will manifest in my interactions with others. I may not want my bitterness about my own life to be forced onto those with whom I interact, but it will seep out of the pores of my body. My resentment toward my life will always come out and poison my relationship with others.

When I heap judgement and violence upon myself, I will always do violence to the people around me. When I am impatient and angry with another, it is because I have been impatient and angry with myself. When I am gentle and accepting toward myself, I will be able to extend gentleness and acceptance toward the other.

Gentleness accepts that the journey of my life has always been about doing the best I could under the circumstances in which I found myself with the skills, abilities, tools, and coping mechanisms available to me at the time. I may have wandered down some peculiar winding ways along the path of life. I may have made choices and decisions that led to pain and chaos for myself and everyone around me. But I was doing the best I could with what I had then.

We do not give a little six-year-old boy a plastic carpenter's tool kit and expect him to go out and build a sixteen-room mansion. He has not got the tools or the skill for the job. The house that I have built with my life is the best house I was able to build with the tools that were in my toolbox at the time. I did the best I could with the skills available to me. In order to be able to embrace others in all their strangeness, I need to embrace within myself those things about myself I find difficult to accept. Richard Rohr writes, "The most courageous thing we will ever do is to bear humbly the mystery of our own reality."[17]

---

17 Richard Rohr, *Everything Belongs: The Gift of Contemplative Prayer* (New York: Crossroad, 1999), p. 84.

In Psalm four the psalmist addresses God, saying, "You gave me room when I was in distress" (Psalm 4:1b). Gentleness grows in spacious places. When we give room for ourselves to be ourselves, we make space for others to be as they truly are. God desires to develop within us that open, expansive place where life can be embraced as it comes to us and others can be welcomed as they are.

No one is excluded. No one is shut out. God opens a spacious place for each of us in all our brokenness, all our confusion, uncertainty, doubt, and pain. God desires us to open a spacious place for ourselves and for one another. When we give ourselves space, light will pour in. When we open up to our true nature created in the image of God, we become more fully the people God created us to be and empower those around us to become more fully the people they were created to be.

The name "Jesus" is the Latin form of the Greek word *Iesous*, which comes from the Hebrew name *Yeshua*, which appears in our English translations of the Hebrew scriptures as Joshua. *Yeshua* is a shortened version of the Hebrew *Yehoshua*, which means saviour or helper. *Yehoshua* can also be translated as "spacious or wide-open plane." So the Hebrew understanding of salvation is to bring us to an open, spacious place.

In Jeremiah 30:7, the prophet describes God's work, saying, "It is a time of distress for Jacob; yet he shall be rescued from it." The word the prophet uses to describe the condition from which Jacob will be rescued is *tsarar*. It means "narrow, constricted, confining." So the work of God is to lead Jacob out of the narrow, constricted place into an expansive open space.

The salvation that *Yeshua*/Jesus came to bring is a wide-open space in which we discover that every part of who we are is embraced by God. Every part of life is held by God. All our struggles, our pain, our brokenness, our wandering ways — they are all held in God's gracious loving care.

This is exactly why Jesus got into so much trouble with the

religious officials of his day. Jesus opened to everyone. Mark the gospel writer says,

> And as he sat at dinner in Levi's house, many tax collectors and sinners were also sitting with Jesus and his disciples — for there were many who followed him. When the scribes of the Pharisees saw that he was eating with sinners and tax collectors, they said to his disciples, "Why does he eat with tax collectors and sinners?" (Mark 2:15–16).

The scribes of the Pharisees at Levi's house lived in a narrow, confined, restricted world. They divided people into those who were in and those who were out. They viewed life in terms of what was deemed acceptable and should be welcomed and what was deemed unacceptable and should be rejected. Jesus created a wide-open place where everyone was welcome. For Jesus, there was no in and no out. Jesus simply opened and embraced whoever came.

In John's gospel, Jesus uses two images to describe his work. He speaks of his ministry in terms of a shepherd leading out his flock and a gatekeeper opening up the gate so that the sheep may follow the shepherd out into the pasture. He says, "The one who enters by the gate is the shepherd of the sheep. The gatekeeper opens the gate for him, and the sheep hear his voice. He calls his own sheep by name and leads them out" (John 10:2–3).

The function of the shepherd/gatekeeper is to make it possible for the sheep to go out of the enclosure into a spacious pasture where they can be fed and protected by the shepherd. The sheep need to know that safety does not lie in the confines of the sheep pen. In fact, Jesus says, the sheep pen is the very place where the thief "climbs in ... to steal and kill and destroy" (John 10:1, 10).

We think safety lies in protecting ourselves, in keeping out the bad things, and building a great wall around our hearts. But

Jesus suggests that, in fact, safety is only found in the wide-open expanse of the pasture where we know we are with the shepherd. Safety comes from letting go of all our securities, surrendering all those things to which we cling that are less than God. The path to gentleness is the path of absolute surrender.

We come to gentleness by letting go of our need for life to be a certain way, our need for answers, understanding, or control. We come to gentleness by laying down our expectations, our need for certain outcomes. We come to gentleness by no longer demanding, clutching, grabbing, clinging, or holding on to anything less than the invisible presence of God's Spirit. Gentleness opens and opens, embracing life as it comes with all its confusion, its dark painful moments, its doubt and trouble.

Everywhere you look in the New Testament you find things being opened. The heavens are opened, the eyes of the blind are opened, the ears of the deaf are opened, mouths that could not speak are opened, graves are opened, gates are opened, prisons are opened, and perhaps above all, hearts are opened. To open means to surrender, to move beyond a life of boundaries and definition, to let go of all those things to which we have ever been attached that are less than God.

Anything to which we cling is a tomb for our spirits. Jesus came to set us free from death, to open to all human beings the possibility of a new way of living. In John chapter eleven, Jesus is shown coming to visit the family of his friend Lazarus who has recently died and been buried. Jesus stands before Lazarus's tomb and tells those gathered around to "Take away the stone" (John 11:39), that is, open the tomb. When they finally move the stone, Jesus calls into the dark cavernous depths where Lazarus's lifeless body has been laid. Jesus cries out, saying, "Lazarus, come out!" (John 11:43).

This is the cry Jesus speaks to each of us. Come out from all those things that bind you to death, from the narrow restricting confines of all the tombs in which you have buried yourself.

Come out from safety, predictability, and understanding, from your need to be in charge of the universe. Come out from your deathly desire to divide the world into acceptable and unacceptable, from all your judgement, condemnation, rejection, hardness of heart toward yourself and others. Come out into the open, spacious place that is the salvation of God.

This is the journey of gentleness. This is the vision God carries for each of our lives. Make room for yourself. You have never been alone. You have never been abandoned. All along the way, the gentle presence of God's Spirit has dwelt within you, leading you on one step at a time.

When you tried to build a great mansion with your little plastic hammer and your toy saw, God watched and understood the great effort you were making to try to build yourself a safe place. God let you build with your own inadequate tools until finally the day came when you knew that your tools were not working any more. And then God watched as you laid aside your tools, letting them go one by one. Until finally the last tool was put aside and you knew that you were not the builder. You knew, that if your life was going to be the life it was created to be, you must surrender every part of it to the one who created it and desires to continue building it.

Then, when finally all your coping mechanisms were gone, when all your excuses had been abandoned, when there was nothing left, Jesus came and "as a hen gathers her brood under her wings" (Matthew 23:37), he drew you into the safe spacious place of his love. This is the place your heart longs to be, the place where gentleness is born. This is the place where you will be empowered by God's gentle Spirit to embrace the other and live in gentleness with all of God's creation.

Discovering Inner Strength

The English version of Paul's list of the fruit of God's Spirit ends with a peculiar conundrum. The final Greek word Paul uses in his list is *egkrateia*. It is almost universally translated as "self-control." The word is used only four other times in the whole New Testament. So there is not a lot of context to support a particular translation. But the idea of "self-control" being a "fruit of the Spirit" makes little sense in the context of Galatians 5:23 or of Christian spiritual teaching.

At the end of his list of the fruit of the Spirit in Galatians 5:22–23, Paul concludes verse 23 by saying, "There is no law against such things." Law and Spirit have nothing to do with each other. Law is about self-effort. The whole point of Galatians is that in Christ we have been set free from the law; we have been liberated from self-effort.

At the beginning of Galatians 5 Paul asserts, "For freedom Christ has set us free." Then he goes on to instruct the Galatians to "Stand firm, therefore, and do not submit again to a yoke of slavery" (Galatians 5:1).

The "yoke of slavery" is the law. The law suggests that it is possible for human beings to measure up to God's standards, improving themselves enough to merit God's favour. In fact, the purpose of the law as Paul understood it was to teach us that we are incapable of keeping the law and to cause us to fall gratefully upon the grace of God who chooses to rescue us from the powers of sin and death. Our rescue comes about not by our self-effort, but by the grace of God at work through God's Spirit in Christ.

Jesus urges his disciples to practise self-denial and self-death, not self-mastery and self-control. "If any want to become my followers, let them deny themselves and take up their cross daily and follow me" (Luke 9:23). "Very truly, I tell you, unless a grain of wheat falls into the earth and dies, it remains just a single grain; but if it dies, it bears much fruit" (John 12:24). The self must die if fruit is to be born. Self-surrender, not self-control, is the Christian path.

Self-control was the virtue of the Pharisees. They practised meticulous law-keeping and exerted profound effort in an attempt to practise the righteousness of God. Jesus pointed out that the Pharisees's self-discipline was so fastidious that they were even careful to tithe the tiniest spices in their kitchens: "you tithe mint, dill, and cummin" (Matthew 23:23). Yet to these self-disciplined religious officials, Jesus says again and again, "Woe to you, scribes and Pharisees" (Matthew 23:13). Even though they believed that their practices were in keeping with the laws of God and their observances were performed in obedience to their understanding of God's will, the Pharisees's careful self-discipline has done them no good.

Paul himself had been the most self-disciplined, law-abiding Pharisee. Yet in his own life he has come to recognize that "self-control" is a complete illusion. In Romans 7, Paul describes his experience, saying, "I do not do what I want, but I do the very thing I hate.... I can will what is right, but I cannot do it. For I do not do the good I want, but the evil I do not want is what I do" (Romans 7:15,18–19). Then Paul cries out in despair, "Wretched man that I am! Who will rescue me from this body of death?" (Romans 7:24).

The answer for Paul is not "I will rescue myself." Paul does not say, "I will redouble my efforts and exercise self-control in order to improve myself." The only answer Paul can offer in his conflicted condition is, "Thanks be to God through Jesus Christ our Lord!" (Romans 7:25). Paul understands that his only hope of becoming the person he was created to be is through God's work in Christ.

Self-effort will never produce the fullness of God's fruit in our lives. We cannot discipline ourselves into a condition that will produce "love, joy, peace, patience, kindness, generosity, faithfulness, [and] gentleness." We can only cast ourselves upon the mercy of God, trusting in God's forgiveness for the unavoidable reality that we frequently fall far short of the glorious vision God has for our lives. We never quite make the mark. If the only response to the awareness of our failure is the counsel that we must redouble our efforts and exert greater self-control, then there is no good news for us in Paul's glorious vision of the Christian life.

The problem with self-control is that it fails to take seriously the complexity of the human condition. At the best of times we humans are a muddle of conflicting emotions, divided loyalties, and perplexing motivations. We spend much of our lives desiring to go in two or more directions at the same time. The illusion of self-control assumes that we know what is best for our lives and will choose to move consistently in the direction of life. Even if human beings did always recognize the best choice, experience indicates that we often fail to choose what is most in tune with the best for ourselves or the rest of the world.

Self-control attempts to order the external circumstances of our lives, in the belief that organizing external reality will bring contentment and peace. Self-control keeps us trapped on the surface, but the fruit of the Spirit are never discovered on the surface.

The fruit of the Spirit are discovered in the deeper part of the human condition, about which Paul speaks in Romans 7, where he draws a contrast between the superficial conflicted self and the deeper inner self that delights in the ways of God. Paul says, "I delight in the law of God in my inmost self, but I see in my members another law" (Romans 7:22–23a). The fruit of God's Spirit is found in our "inmost self." It is precisely this "inmost self" that the ninth and final fruit of the Spirit addresses.

In fruit number nine, Paul is not instructing us to take control of our lives. He is instructing us to find our deeper self and trust that, in this deeper self, there is a reality and strength that comes to us as a gift of God's Spirit.

The Greek word *enkrateia*, which is commonly translated as "self-control," is a compound word consisting of two Greek words: *en*, which means "in," and *kratos*, which means "strength." So the word literally means "in strength." A much better translation than "self-control" would be "strength within" or "inner strength." Paul's final fruit of the Spirit is the quality of inner strength that comes from opening to the presence and power of God dwelling within our innermost being.

Human beings long to find "inner strength." We long to discover within ourselves a strength we know that, on our own, we lack. We know we are not capable of exercising adequate self-control in order to always manifest the fruit of God's Spirit. Jesus made this point over and over in the "Sermon on the Mount," when he took the normal requirements of the law and expanded them to impossible proportions. Jesus said, "You have heard that it was said, 'You shall not commit adultery.' But I say to you that everyone who looks at a woman with lust has already committed adultery with her in his heart" (Matthew 5:27–28).

The point is not to pile a burden of guilt upon those who have failed to fulfill this high standard for human conduct. Jesus wants us to recognize the limitations of our human resources. He calls us to seek a power that is greater than our own limited ability to fulfill the extraordinary vision for which we were created. Jesus pushes us to the limits of human ability in order that we might discover an inner strength we never knew we had.

My daughter recently travelled alone to Europe. She is a

quiet young woman, not inclined to wild adventure. She had never really been away from home alone. As we watched her walk through the gates at the airport to board a plane to London, her mother and I felt some anxiety. We believed deeply that our daughter had within her a strength she had never been called upon to fully utilize. But we were not sure that she was aware of this strength within herself.

Our daughter's European tour unfolded with relatively minor drama until she arrived in the train station in Rome. At the best of times Rome is a noisy, busy, intimidating city. For a young woman all alone it can be an almost overwhelming challenge. Immediately she stepped off the train in Rome our daughter was approached by an old man demanding she give him money. When she refused, he slapped her across the face and threw her down on the train platform. No one came to her aid. No one helped her get up and gather her belongings together. No one asked if she was okay. Stunned and scraped, she pulled herself to her feet and managed to carry on with her journey. Alone in a foreign and threatening environment, she discovered within herself a strength she had never known she possessed.

For the writer of the Letter to the Ephesians the gift of discovering this inner strength is the only thing we really need in order to fulfill God's call in our lives. In Ephesians chapter three, the writer prays for his audience that God

> according to the riches of his glory ... may grant that you may be strengthened in your inner being with power through his Spirit, and that Christ may dwell in your hearts through faith, as you are being rooted and grounded in love. I pray that you may have the power to comprehend, with all the saints, what is the breadth and length and height and depth, and to know the love of Christ that surpasses knowledge, so that you may be filled with all the fullness of God (Ephesians 3:16–19).

Strength is found "in your inner being." It is not something we can manufacture ourselves; it is given "through his Spirit," as Christ dwells in our "hearts through faith."

As with all of the fruit of God's Spirit, we grow in inner strength when we trust in the One who produces the fruit. The more we trust God's Spirit, the more God's strength will grow within us. God calls us not to self-control, but to self-surrender. We are called to surrender our wills to God's Spirit, to listen deeply within and respond to the word of strength we discover within ourselves. Surrender is the path to strength.

Cynthia Bourgeault writes, "Far from an act of spiritual cowardice, surrender is an act of spiritual power because it opens the heart directly to the more subtle realms of spiritual Wisdom and energy."[18] Surrender unlocks the power of God's Spirit to produce God's fruit and to guide us into the paths of God's righteousness.

God does not, however, provide strength to do those things God is not directing us to do. Often we want strength to fulfill our agendas rather than to produce God's fruit. We want energy and power in order to make a big impression on the world, to become famous, wealthy, or powerful. If this is our destiny, we will be granted God's strength to fulfill this calling.

More likely, we are called to the ordinary routine tasks of life — to love and care for those among whom we live; to demonstrate "love, joy, peace, patience, kindness, generosity, faithfulness, [and] gentleness" with all people we encounter. God will always provide the strength for us to love. The energy to bring peace and to exercise patience, kindness, and generosity will always be present for those who live in Christ and trust in God's Spirit.

---

18 Cynthia Bourgeault, *The Wisdom Way of Knowing: Reclaiming an Ancient Tradition to Awaken the Heart* (San Francisco: Jossey-Bass, 2003), p. 73.

God never asks us to do or be anything for which God has not provided the inner strength. The challenge is not to find a way to be more loving, joyful, peaceful, patient, kind, generous, faithful, or gentle. It is to identify in our lives those things we are pursuing that are not directed by God's Spirit and to let them go, so that we might find the inner strength that comes from following where God's Spirit is leading.

Before she left on her European trip, I asked my daughter why she was going. She replied, "I don't really know. This is just something that I know I have to do." Such knowing comes from God's Spirit. And whenever we follow the knowing that comes from God's Spirit, we will be given the strength and the resources necessary to fulfill the call of that knowing.

God does not call us to self-control or self-discipline. God calls us to deep listening. Self-control and self-discipline belong to the law, and law brings only death. Life comes from God's Spirit. Those who hear and follow where God's Spirit leads will find within themselves the strength and power of God's Spirit. When we live in tune with the Spirit of God, we will find the fruit of the Spirit spontaneously emerging from within.

Living in tune with God's Spirit is the only path to "love, joy, peace, patience, kindness, generosity, faithfulness, gentleness, and inner strength."

A Fruitful Struggle

It would be a serious mistake to think that manifesting the fruit of the Spirit is an easy task. The nine fruit of the Spirit that Paul lists constitute an extraordinary and challenging vision. Paul makes it depressingly clear in Galatians five that he is under no illusion about the significant struggle living by the Spirit will always be. Paul is not a starry-eyed idealist in his assessment of the human condition. He understands that we humans are often deeply complex and conflicted beings.

In Galatians five, Paul describes the human condition, saying, "What the flesh desires is opposed to the Spirit, and what the Spirit desires is opposed to the flesh; for these are opposed to each other, to prevent you from doing what you want" (Galatians 5:17). The opposition here is not between body and Spirit, as if our bodies were the source of the conflict. Paul is not the body-hating ascetic he has sometimes been accused of being. The opposition is between "flesh" and Spirit. There is within each of us a dimension of our being Paul calls "flesh."

"Flesh," as Paul calls it here in Galatians, is that part of ourselves which opposes God's Spirit. "Flesh" is centred on the self and wants only one thing. It is determined to get its way no matter what the cost. This "flesh" is an actual power at work within us. The original Greek of Galatians 5:17 gives more of an active agency to "flesh" than is suggested by the *New Revised Standard Version*. Paul is saying here that "flesh lusts against the Spirit." It is actively working against God's Spirit. "Flesh" is determined to lead us away from God, to destroy our awareness of God's presence that is the source of all life and hope.

This battle may not always look as dark and as terrible as we sometimes think. Many of the "works of the flesh" Paul lists in Galatians 5:19–21 are quite ordinary. We have probably all, at times, fallen victim to "enmity" or participated in creating a little bit of "strife." There are not many human beings who have not, occasionally, fallen prey to "jealousy, anger, quarrels, dissensions, factions," and "envy." And just in case we feel we cannot find our particular weakness in the list of fifteen characteristic "works of the flesh," Paul concludes by adding, "and things like these." There is room for any honest person in this list. None of us is ever entirely free of "the works of the flesh" in this life.

Over the past twenty-five years of ordained ministry I have heard quite a bit of fairly honest talk. People tell me things from time to time that in some cases they may never have told another living human being. And in all that honest talk, I have discovered one thing that is universally true. It does not matter how successful your life may look on the surface or how strong, healthy, or beautiful you may be. Everyone struggles with life. I have never met one person who has said to me, "I am exactly the person I want to be." No one has ever come to me and acknowledged, "There is not one single tiny thing about myself that I would change if I had the power to change it."

It seems to be part of the human condition that we are conflicted beings. Spending time reflecting on the fruit of the Spirit can make our awareness of this disconnect, between who we know ourselves to be and who we would like to be, seem even greater. So what are we to do in response to our awareness that we all fall short of the vision God has for our lives?

One option is to spend the rest of our lives beating ourselves up about our terrible failure. This is a sadly common option, particularly among Christians. We see things in ourselves that are not as we wish they were, and we draw the conclusion that we are terribly unworthy people. If I could expunge one word from the Christian vocabulary it would be the word *should*. "I should do this or I should not do that. I should be better. I should not feel this way. I should not act this way." When I spend my life *shoulding* myself, all I do is shut myself down.

Should will never open me to that broader more expansive place in my being where God is known. When we spend our lives obsessing about our shortcomings, it is difficult to soften and open to a deeper awareness of God's presence.

But there is another approach. Instead of being overwhelmed by the distance between the vision God has for our lives and the reality we see in ourselves, we need to take encouragement from the awareness that, apart from Jesus, no human being has ever perfectly fulfilled the vision of life for which we were designed. Seeing our failures needs to challenge us not to beat ourselves up, but to be honest about the reality of our human condition. Christians are not little plastic saints with all our colours nicely painted on and our hair always perfectly coiffed. We are all a bit of a mess from time to time. And our spiritual journey will only be hampered by pretending this is not true.

Jesus said, "Those who are well have no need of a physician, but those who are sick ... I have come to call not the righteous but sinners" (Matthew 9:12, 13b). And Paul says, "all have sinned and fall short of the glory of God" (Romans 3:23). The only people who ever find themselves outside the grace and mercy of God are those who have come to the conclusion that they have no need for God's grace. If you think you can do it on your own, God will let you try.

There is something broken in us. We need to know that we cannot fix this brokenness ourselves. We do not measure up. But this is not our primary problem. The main difficulty arises when we start to look at our shortcomings and believe that this is all there is to say about us. We need to find a way to hold together the reality of our flawed humanity, our powerlessness to fix it, and the extraordinarily exalted vision God has for our lives.

James Finley, trying to describe the power he experienced in Thomas Merton says,

> We might put it this way: the master limps, but the master is not handicapped by the limping. Why are we handicapped by our limping? Because we believe our limping has the power to name what we are. Our limping fills us with shame. We wish that we didn't have to limp anymore. We hope that others don't notice it too much and all of that. The master limps perhaps as much or more than you do; but the master knows that that is not the point. The master knows it's just limping — why be handicapped by it?[19]

The key to accepting our limping lies in the short statement Paul makes right after he concludes his list of the fruit of the Spirit. In Galatians 5:24, Paul declares, "And those who belong to Christ Jesus have crucified the flesh with its passions and desires." The heart of this verse is the four Greek words, *hoi de tou Christou* — "and they that are the Christ's." If we are going to live at peace with the struggle of the human condition, we need to know to whom it is we belong. Paul says we belong to Christ. We are "*tou Christou*," the Christ's. No matter what may happen in our lives, we belong to Christ.

No matter how twisted and confused we may become, no matter what we have done in the past or may do in the future, the truth remains — we belong to Christ. We are not named by our "limping"; we are named by Christ.

We have been given a new identity. It is an identity that does not depend on doing things right or getting the right answers

---

19   James Finley, "In the Presence of a Master," *Thomas Merton's Path to the Palace of Nowhere*, an audio series printed in *Radical Grace*, vol. 16, no. 1, January–March, 2003.

or always behaving properly and piously. Our identity depends entirely upon what God has done for us in Christ. We belong to Christ not because we are such fine examples of the fruit of God's Spirit but because Christ has claimed us as his own. And because we belong to Christ, we have everything we need.

In 1 Corinthians 3:21–23, Paul says,

> So let no one boast about human leaders. For all things are yours, whether Paul or Apollos or Cephas or the world or life or death or the present or the future – all belong to you, and you belong to Christ, and Christ belongs to God.

Because you belong to Christ, "all things are yours," everything "belongs to you." The common thread of the works of the flesh, listed in Galatians 5:19–21, is that they all stem from the perception that something is lacking in us. They arise from a sense of emptiness. We indulge in the works of the flesh because we feel that life is not rewarding us adequately; we have missed out on something. So we are going to go and get that something and make it happen in our lives. This is the work of the flesh.

The fruit of the Spirit will emerge naturally and spontaneously when we know that in Christ we have come to the end of all human need. There is no longer any lack in our being. We do not have to get anything. Life as it is, at this very moment, is entirely adequate. When we know that, if nothing were to change from this moment, it would be okay, then something deep within us opens up. We begin to discover that, beneath the struggle, there is "love."

Deeper than the turmoil, pain, uncertainty, and insecurity that so often characterize the surface of life, there is "joy." When we finally stop needing to get something out of life, we discover that, beneath the surface tension of wanting and grasping, peace begins to emerge. When we no longer need people to be a certain way in order to meet our needs, instead of "strife, jealousy, anger, quarrels, dissensions, factions, envy," we find "patience, kindness, generosity, faithfulness, gentleness." When we come to the end of our striving and simply accept that where we are is where we are meant to be, we find "inner strength" present at the heart of our being.

It is not that we produce these qualities within ourselves. It is simply that, as we focus on the reality of who we are and on the presence of Christ within us, we find that there is a deeper reality. It is not even that all the works of the flesh immediately drop away. There will still be times when we find "things like these" in our behaviour. But we will know to whom it is we belong and, therefore, we will know that there is something more true about us than the sad broken behaviour we may see at times in our lives.

Paul's list of the fruit of the Spirit is not intended to be one more stick we use to beat ourselves up with. The struggle of the Christian life is not to make ourselves better people or to fix our brokenness. The struggle of the Christian life is to be deeply honest about who we are and, at the same time, to hold absolutely to the most exalted vision of human behaviour that we find in Christ. The next stage is to know that, when we fall short of this standard, we continue to belong to Christ.

When Jesus was attacked by his own people, he said, "My sheep hear my voice. I know them, and they follow me. I give them eternal life, and they will never perish. No one will snatch them out of my hand" (John 10:27–28).

The key is to stay connected to the voice that tells us the truth. The first thing Paul says, when he launches out into the contrast between "the works of the flesh" and the "fruit of the Spirit," is "Live by the Spirit, I say, and do not gratify the desires of the flesh" (Galatians 5:16). This is a rather unfortunate translation. What Paul actually says is, "Walk in the Spirit, I say, and you will not fulfill the desires of the flesh." Stay connected to the Spirit, stay in God, and the rest will take care of itself.

You do not have to beat yourself up. You do not have to discipline yourself. You do not have to exert your energy and determination. You need only to stay connected. Stay open to the gentle presence of God's Spirit within, and God's Spirit will produce the fruit. God's Spirit will form and shape your life so that you become, increasingly, the person you were created to be. This is God's promise. This is the Christian path of the spiritual life.

When he was physically present with his disciples on earth, Jesus said to them, "I am the vine, you are the branches" (John 15:5). The same sap, the same life force, the same Spirit that ran through Jesus' body during his earthly life, is present in you now. So Jesus says, simply, "Abide in me as I abide in you. Just as the branch cannot bear fruit by itself unless it abides in the vine, neither can you unless you abide in me" (John 15:4).

Fruit comes from being connected. Stay away from those things that cause you to lose your awareness of the intimate connection between you and Christ in God's Spirit. Find those things in your life that deepen and refresh your awareness of this vital life-giving connection. Then, no matter what struggle you face, the fruit will unfold in your life.

Conclusion: Growing God's Fruit

At the beginning of our examination of the fruit of the Spirit, I noted the danger that, having described how a Christian life might look, we might then turn that description into a set of rules by which we attempt to govern our external behaviour. Most people would like to display more of the fruit of the Spirit in their lives. If we heard of a workshop guaranteeing to make us more generous, faithful, gentle, and kind, we would probably all sign up. But focusing on these qualities and striving to attain them is exactly the wrong approach.

The fruit of the Spirit are not the fruit of self-effort, determination, hard work, or self-discipline. They are the fruit of God's Holy Spirit working in a person's life to produce the nature and characteristics that demonstrate the reality of God's presence. It is important in any discussion of the fruit of God's Spirit to always keep in mind the relationship between the person in whom the fruit is produced and the Holy Spirit who is the fruit producer.

The New Testament uses a number of images to speak about the work of God's Holy Spirit. One of the strongest pictures of the work of the Spirit is in John 20:19–23. Jesus has just appeared to Mary Magdalene, who has reported to the disciples, "I have seen the Lord" (John 20:18). In the evening of the same day they heard Mary's report, Jesus' disciples are hiding together in a house with the doors locked "for fear of the Jews" (John 20:19).

It is not hard to find ourselves in company with these disciples. A look at Paul's list of the fruit of God's Spirit might cause anyone to feel a little paralysed. If the Christian vision for our lives is that we might always be loving, joyful, peaceful, patient, kind, generous, faithful, gentle, and filled with inner strength, we may feel a little overwhelmed and stuck. Most of us will be conscious that we fall short of the goal. It is tempting to join Jesus' disciples, lock the doors, and hide from the challenges that confront us.

But the story as John tells it, clarifies the fact that we cannot hide from Jesus. Jesus ignores the locked doors and comes and stands among his fearful disciples, shows them his wounds, and reassures them with words of God's peace. He commissions them to go out into the world. Then John says, Jesus "breathed on them and said to them, 'Receive the Holy Spirit' " (John 20:22).

When we read this description of Jesus breathing on his disciples, we are intended to hear an echo from the book of Genesis where, describing the creation of human beings, the writer says, "then the Lord God formed man from the dust of the ground, and breathed into his nostrils the breath of life; and the man became a living being" (Genesis 2:7). Genesis shows the creation of human beings occurring in two stages. It begins with the physical creation: "The Lord God formed man from the dust of the ground." At this point there is still no life. Only when God "breathed into his nostrils the breath of life" did "man [become] a living being."

Three hundred years before Jesus lived, Jewish scholars in Alexandria, Egypt, translated into Greek the Hebrew scriptures we now know as the Old Testament. In Genesis 2:7 they translated the Hebrew word *naphach*, which in English is "breathed," into the Greek word *emphusao*. This is the same Greek word the writer of John's gospel used to describe what Jesus did to the disciples when he encountered them in hiding.

Just as God had originally breathed life into the lifeless material formed from the dust of the earth, so now Jesus breathes life into his lifeless, paralysed disciples who have been entombed in their fears. Jesus is sending his disciples out into the world to proclaim the victory of life over death. But first they must come to life themselves. They must have within themselves that creative life-giving power of God that is God's Holy Spirit. Only then are they equipped to live the life to which they are called.

In this passage John is suggesting that in Christ humanity has been recreated. A kind of second creation has taken place. Humanity has been redeemed, made new, and recreated through Christ. In the resurrection, death has been overcome and life has been restored. The process of the fall has been reversed. In a new and dramatic way the Holy Spirit of life has been released on earth and in the lives of human beings. The bars of the cosmic prison that had been forged by human sin have been burst. The stone of death has been rolled away from the mouth of the tomb. Life has been set free.

In Christ humankind has been restored to its original purpose to be in intimate, dynamic living relationship with God. The fruit of God's Spirit is a picture of what that relationship will look like, and the Holy Spirit is the power by which that picture will be fulfilled.

The Holy Spirit is the power of life, the power of love, the force by which all of life has come into existence. When Jesus breathed on his disciples, he was saying to them, "This force lives in you. This power that originally brought all of life into existence actually dwells within your being. This Spirit that created everything at the beginning of time is at work in your life in this present moment. This Holy Spirit of God is teaching, guiding, leading, nurturing, supporting, and feeding you."

We need to know that this is not just true historically for Jesus' first disciples. This is a living reality today. The Holy Spirit of God dwells within us. Jesus has breathed upon us the breath of life, and God's Spirit is present in our beings. We do not need to go in search of God. We do not need to find anything or go anywhere apart from where we are. God is here with us; God is here within us.

The Holy Spirit is God dwelling in our lives, the power of

God shaping us, forming us into the extraordinary beings we were created to be. God is in fact at work in our lives making us into the loving, joyful, peaceful, patient, kind, generous, faithful, gentle, strong beings we were created to be. This is who we are. This is a vision of our lives as we were designed to be. Our task is to allow God to recreate us into the original vision God has for our lives.

We are not powerless victims. As Paul says, "your body is a temple of the Holy Spirit within you, which you have from God" (1 Corinthians 6:19). There really is nothing much more you need to know about yourself. You are a container of divinity. You are a vessel of God's presence. There is nothing you need to get, nothing you need to accomplish, achieve, or prove. God's Spirit lives in you. You are a carrier of the power that brought Jesus back from death to life. And this power is always available in the depths of your being, re-forming you into the original image of God in which you were first created.

It is important, however to remember that, in this process we do have a part to play. As Jesus breathes God's Spirit into his disciples, he says to them, "Receive the Holy Spirit." The Greek word translated "receive" is *lambano. Lambano* is a complicated Greek word with a variety of potential nuances. The basic meaning of this verb is "to take." But it can also imply the more passive action of receiving. If it is used to speak about a transaction between two people, it implies one person opening to another or one person allowing another to have access to their lives. If I receive you, I am opening myself to you. I am allowing you into my life. I am making myself vulnerable to you.

In John chapter 20, Jesus is instructing his disciples to give the Holy Spirit full access to their lives. He is calling them to open to the presence of life in God's Spirit. Jesus is asking his disciples to allow him to open the locked doors of their hearts and to replace their fears with his peace. He is encouraging them to allow their lives to be shaped by God's Spirit. The active agent in this story is Jesus. The active agent in our lives is God's Holy Spirit. We do not have to create the fruit of God's Spirit. We simply need to give God access to our whole lives and allow God to do the work within us that God desires to do. We need only to let go of any obstacles that hinder the fullness of God's work.

This is why he breathed God's Spirit on his disciples and instructed them to open to God's presence. Jesus sums up the path to continued fruitfulness by saying, "If you forgive the sins of any, they are forgiven them; if you retain the sins of any, they are retained" (John 20:23). This has been a puzzling and much misused statement. What Jesus is saying is both simpler and more universal than has often been understood.

In this passage the word translated as "forgive" is the Greek word *aphiemi*. It does mean "forgive," but it also has a much broader meaning — simply "to let go." So the first part of verse 23 could be translated, "Whoever's sins you let go, they are let go" or "released."

The opposite statement in the second half of the verse uses the Greek word *krateo*, translated as "retain," which can also mean "hold fast," "take hold of," or "bind." This would lead to a translation of the second half of the verse saying, "Whoever's sins you hold fast, they will continue to be bound." The principle is that anything we let go brings freedom into our lives and releases freedom into all of creation. When we choose to let go of whatever hinders God's work, we allow God's ongoing process of creation to continue.

We are being invited to enter into the creative process of God through the power of God's Holy Spirit. We enter this process by letting go of those things that cripple and ensnare us, by releasing our fears, and by opening the locked cages in which we have lived. When we let go of those things that have hindered God's work, we discover that the fragrance of God's Spirit is also released. God's Spirit smells like "love, joy, peace, patience, kindness, generosity, faithfulness, gentleness, and inner strength."

In the very next verse (Galatians 5:23) Paul continues by saying, "There is no law against such things." On the other hand, these qualities cannot be produced by law. They will never come about in our lives as a result of self-effort. The fruit of God's Spirit will only ever be produced in a life that is fully and deeply surrendered to the working of God's Spirit. The Holy Spirit is free to work in and through us when we stop binding, holding, grasping, clutching, and fighting for things to be as we believe they ought to be. God's Spirit is free to work in our lives when we open to the Spirit and release ourselves into God's care and guidance.

There is a lovely little parable that has been used in spiritual teaching for many years. The version I like best is told by Cynthia Bourgeault in her book *The Wisdom Way of Knowing*. I have slightly adapted Cynthia's version.

> Once upon a time in a land in the West, there was a kingdom of acorns living at the foot of a towering old oak tree. Since the citizens of this kingdom were modern fully Westernized acorns, they lived reasonably and sensibly with focused energy and purposeful discipline. Since the inhabitants of this acorn kingdom were midlife, baby-boomer acorns, they bought shelves of self-help books and participated in regular workshops to become the best acorns they could be. They took seminars on "Getting All You Can Out of Your Shell." They had support groups for acorns who had been bruised in their original fall from the tree and recovery groups for acorns raised in dysfunctional families. There were spas for oiling and polishing their shells and various acornopathic therapies to enhance life expectancy and well-being.
>
> One day in the midst of this busy kingdom of acorns, a stranger suddenly appeared. He was dirty and his shell was cracked, making an immediate negative impression

on all the other nice well-groomed acorns. The visitor sat beneath the oak tree and told a crazy tale. Looking upward at the great oak tree towering above, he said, "We ... are ... that!"

"Ridiculous!" the other acorns concluded. "How could a tiny acorn possibly be a great oak tree reaching twenty metres into the air?" But one persistent acorn questioned the visitor: "So tell us," the inquisitive acorn asked, "how could we become that?" "Well" said the visitor, "there are two things. First, you need to trust that the power to become a great oak has been given to you and is trapped inside your shell. And then," he went on looking down at the ground, "in order for that power that is in you to be released to become the tree, you have to let go of all your schemes and plans for your life and go down into the ground ... where your shell will crack open and that power that is in you will be released."

"Insane," all the acorns cried together, "Why, then we would no longer be acorns."[20]

Paul's list of the fruit of God's Spirit is a description of our true nature. In our truest self, created in the image of God, we are loving, joyful, peaceful, patient, kind, generous, faithful, gentle, strong beings. This is who we are. It may not be the way we most often view ourselves. It may not even be the way most of us behave much of the time.

But Jesus has breathed into us the Spirit of "love, joy, peace, patience, kindness, generosity, faithfulness, gentleness, and inner

---

20 Adapted from Cynthia Bourgeault, *The Wisdom Way of Knowing: Reclaiming an Ancient Tradition to Awaken the Heart* (San Francisco: Jossey-Bass, 2003), p. 64.

strength." So to the degree that we give God's Spirit free reign in our lives, we will discover these qualities coming to the surface and manifesting in our behaviour. We do not have to work at this. We have only to work at letting go of the distractions that hinder God's work in our being.

As we accept our destiny to die in Christ, we are reborn by the God's Spirit in the image of God. The fruit we have explored give us a picture of what that reborn life looks like. These fruit will grow in our lives to the degree that we surrender fully and deeply to the Spirit of God who has been breathed into our lives.

Path Books
A LIGHT TO MY PATH

We hope that you have enjoyed reading this Path Book. For more information about Path Books, please visit our website at **www.pathbooks.com**. If you have coments or suggestions about Path Books, please write us at <u>publisher@pathbooks.com</u>.

Christ Wisdom: Spiritual Practice in the Beatitudes and the Lord's Prayer by Christopher Page
The Beatitudes and the Lord's Prayer offer us a profound challenge to live in intimate communion with God. This pastorally oriented book aims to helps us discover new insights in Jesus' teaching. Each chapter includes reflective questions and spiritual exercises to help integrate the teachings into everyday life.
1-55126-420-X soft cover, 160 pages, $16.95

Mark's Gospel: Awakening the Voice Within
by Christopher Page
The words of Mark's gospel turn a searching light into the souls of its readers, enabling us to examine our hearts, question our assumptions, and seek God's truth in our lives. Taking these words seriously, Page proposes, will change our lives in deep ways. Includes questions for journaling or discussion.
1-55126-450-1 soft cover, 184 pages, $19.95

The Way of Courage: Being God's People in a Broken World
by Christopher Page
How do God's people respond to difficult situations? Do we choose confrontation and wounding, or reconciliation and healing? By being the people we are, we create the community we belong to. Suggestions for personal exploration and group study accompany each reflection.
1-55126-479-X soft cover, 166 pages, $19.95

Finer than Gold, Sweeter than Honey: The Psalms for Our Living by Herbert O'Driscoll
The psalms are among the most sublime poetry in the world, offering us inexhaustible wells of meaning. Herbert O'Driscoll dips into their sacred depths and draws up sparkling insights to refresh the soul. The reader will find rewarding suggestions for personal reflection, daily journalling, group discussion, or sermon preparation.
1-55126-449-8 soft cover, 309 pages, $26.95

Four Days in Spring: Christ Suffering, Dying, and Rising in Our Lives by Herbert O'Driscoll
In twenty-four poignant reflections, Herbert O'Driscoll vividly recreates the biblical story, taking us into the hearts and minds of the characters. He then returns to our own time and place, guiding us to find — as they did — an infinite Source of strength in moments of sorrow, pain, or loss; and eternal hope for living. Far from being an ending, those four days in spring were a beginning of what would become the gift of Christianity and the community of faith we call the church.
1-55126-493-5 soft cover, 111 pages, $16.95